DISRUPTORS
OF
Harmony

———

TONYA MASELLI, LICSW

Disruptors of Harmony

Visit our website at
www.StillwaterPress.com
for more information.
First Stillwater River Publications Edition
ISBN: 978-1-955123-31-0
1 2 3 4 5 6 7 8 9 10
Written by Tonya Maselli
Published by Stillwater River Publica-
tions,
Pawtucket, RI, USA.
Publisher's Cataloging-In-Publication Data
(Prepared by The Donohue Group, Inc.)

Names: Maselli, Tonya, author.
Title: Disruptors of harmony / Tonya Ma-
    selli, LICSW.
Description: First Stillwater River Publica-
    tions edition. | Pawtucket, RI, USA :
    Stillwater River Publications, [2021]
Identifiers: ISBN 9781955123310
Subjects: LCSH: Stress management. | Stress
    (Psychology)--Social aspects. | Harmony
    (Philosophy) | LCGFT: Self-help publica-
    tions.
Classification: LCC RA785 .M37 2021 | DDC
    155.9042--dc23

Don't stop, keep striving,
do not be discouraged,
don't let anything hold you back
until you get to a point
when you GIVE UP on giving up.

-Torah
Taopheeq Yousuph

Dedicated to GOD first and foremost.

To my daughter, Ava for your constant inspiration with your steady stream of kindness and laughter. To my parents, family, friends and Glen for your love and support through all my struggles and successes. Thank you for helping me restore my harmony in times of need. I also dedicate this book to anyone who may be facing life's struggles. You are not alone, and I wish you the strength to see it through with peace and tranquility.

Table of Contents

Introduction

Stressors surround us as we move hastily through our daily lives. Many seek harmony and inner peace yet seldom achieve their objectives. Unavoidable circumstances may interfere with reaching desired goals. Sadly, life seems to be getting more difficult for most individuals. The *Little House on the Prairie* days, while burdensome, represented simplistic times. For many, this contributed to a more settled way of living. Past family life appeared more intact. Life today seems distant and disconnected. We have come so far in our advancements and technologies, yet we have gone nowhere. Everything has a price.

Socialization seems stunted or nonexistent. Suicide and homelessness rates are high. Perhaps the price of present-day society is the disruption of harmony. Identifying what may stand in the way of one's peace of mind and tranquility may begin the much-needed dialogue.

Combining this with clinical perspective, positive affirmations, and words of wisdom by historical figures, as well as resources and stories of overcoming adversity, may lead us to a more tranquil way of life.

Today, the United States appears to be an overly stressed society.

Perhaps we have always been, but nowadays – we just may discuss and analyze it more. Stress and a lack of harmony may run hand in hand. Stress may have a negative impact on our health and therefore, it is important to better understand stressors and work toward alleviating them. Once this happens, we are able to restore harmony by understanding stress connections. Let us journey back about fifty years ago. Personally, the 1970's provided me with a carefree and fun childhood. I wasn't stressed or worried about potential attacks by crazed individuals. Perhaps I was sheltered, or perhaps it was truly a calmer existence. I realize I owe much of this to my wonderful parents. My home life was a beautiful one, for which I am most grateful. I also have terrific friends, some of whom have been a part of my life since childhood. These great individuals have provided me with security and support during the good and bad times. This is especially important for alleviating stress in one's life. Support systems contribute to coping mechanisms. One must not feel alone in this world.

Whether it be a connection spiritually, culturally, or otherwise, one must feel a connection outside of one's self. Even if that connection is with just one person, that is all it takes.

If you are someone who may negatively state, "I don't have many friends," consider if you have just one friend. If so, that is all you need. It takes just one true friend to help you through life's difficulties and stressful times. It is important to have trust in that friendship. Allow yourself to reach out for help when you need it, and reciprocate by being there for your friend when he/she is in need.

Empathy, loyalty, kindness, consideration, and respect are the key components of a healthy friendship. The concept of stress discussed for the purposes of this book refers to the overall life stress within the United States culture. Topics will be identified that stand in the way of one's peace of mind and tranquility. Clinical perspective, positive affirmations, and quotations by notable figures, as well as resources and stories about overcoming adversity will be included. No one is exempt from life's struggles.

We will uncover what stands in the way of harmony, and discuss ways to move forward productively. Throughout this book, you will find quotations by various authors. It is important to note that no one particular individual is being promoted. Some may agree or disagree with those quoted within this book. There are many worthwhile individuals throughout history who should be referenced and remembered, but unfortunately we were not able to include all of them. Those chosen have made some great noteworthy contributions. Some of their struggles may even help us move forward with our own. It is important that we continue to encourage positivity in our lives. For this purpose, we will move forward with confidence so that all may express themselves and feel empowered. Please visit the website ALEGEEMPOWER.COM to further explore positive words, services and products. Alege, pronounced ul-ee-g, is a Romanian word meaning "to choose". It is your choice to embrace positivity and positive affirmations. Your choice may lead to empowerment. If you choose to visit ALEGEEMPOWER.COM, feel free to share these positive words or quotes with others. Please note that this book serves as a guide and in no way is meant to clinically diagnose medical and/or mental health issues. Please seek professional help if any medical and/or psychiatric conditions are in question for yourself, a friend, or a loved one.

It is important to note that Disruptors of Harmony was written prior to the Covid-19 Pandemic and death of George Floyd. Great devastation has been experienced throughout the world. We continue to struggle with illness, isolation, and sadness surrounding the loss of loved ones and changes within our society. Many remain hopeful and this we continue to see by witnessing acts of kindness, medical professionals assisting ill patients and their families, neighbors helping one another, continued peaceful protests for the senseless killing of Mr. Floyd, and a continued fight for equal rights and treatment of all. The content and message of this book remains the same. No one is exempt from life's struggles and we are all in this together. We must not give up the fight for ourselves and others.

Chapter One
Stress

"STRESS - A physical, chemical, or emotional factor that causes bodily or mental tension and may be a factor in disease causation."[1]

Let us restore...harmony and affection without which liberty and even life itself are but dreary things.[2]
— Thomas Jefferson (1801)

Thomas Jefferson was the third president of the United States of America, and the author of the Declaration of Independence. It is important to also state that he was a slave owner. This book is not about judgement and disgrace, but rather a discussion

---

[1] Merriam-Webster.Com Dictionary, 2019.

[2] Jefferson, Thomas, March 4, 1801. University of Virginia Press. First Inaugural Address in Founders.archives.gov.

about the past, present, and future – for a better understanding. As my dear friend Desi likes to quote the words of Sir Francis Bacon: "knowledge is power".[3] Let us consider our history to better understand our current day circumstances. Thomas Jefferson was asking to bring back balance and fondness because without it, our freedom and existence would be bleak. Has much changed since Thomas Jefferson spoke those words? Slavery existed during that time. Today, people continue to fight for their freedoms and rights. Harmony may not exist for those held captive. *Disruptors of Harmony* will look at current daily stressors which may affect our lives and impact our peace of mind and tranquility. We will consider different coping mechanisms along this journey as well.

Disruptors of Harmony will put a plan of action in place to help you combat worries and stressors. Let us begin by going back in time over thirty-five years ago. According to the June 6, 1983 edition of *Time* Magazine's, "Stress: Can We Cope?," Sixty-six percent of family physician appointments were related to stress.[4] This number continued to climb and jumped considerably over the next few years. Beth Israel Deaconess Medical Center, a Harvard Medical School

---

[3] Bacon, Francis. Brainyquote.com, 2019.

[4] Wallis, et al, Stress: Can We Cope?, June 6, 1983. Vol. 121 No. 23.

Teaching Hospital, published "Stress Management Counseling in the Primary Care Setting is Rare" in 2012. The article states that sixty to eighty percent of primary care visits may relate to stress; however, only a small percentage of patients – under five percent – actually receive stress management counseling.[5]

I have witnessed the stress of individuals while working as a social worker practicing in primary care settings and hospital environments. A physician colleague approached me years ago to set up a clinical counseling office within his practice space. This was unique, and often not found in most primary care settings. He was discovering more and more patients in need of psychotherapy services, which allowed patients an opportunity to be seen the same day as their primary care appointment if warranted. Each week, I was busy meeting with patients following their appointments with their providers. It seemed helpful to both clients and physicians. It also allowed a warm hand off from physician to clinician – which appeared to alleviate anxieties with patients.

A 2013 HuffPost Healthy Living article by author Joe Robinson, "Three-Quarters of Your Doctor Bills are Because of This," indicates that stress is found to

---

[5] Nerurkar,et al, Stress Management Counseling in the Primary Care Setting is Rare, Beth Deaconess Medical Center (2012, November 19).

be a contributing factor in the top five leading causes of death. Leading causes of death included accidents, cancer, heart disease, lower respiratory disease, and stroke. The article also estimates that primary care visits relating to stress were between seventy-five and ninety percent.[6] We continue to witness the increase in stress-related primary care visits.

The Miami Herald published an article in 2014 by Deborah S. Hartz-Seeley, "Chronic Stress is Linked to the Six Leading Causes of Death". Ms. Hartz-Seeley included suicide among the leading causes of death as well.[7] Therefore, chronic stress is a contributing factor to the top leading causes of death.

Let us return to the 1983 Time Magazine article, "Stress: Can We Cope?". The article also references stress connected with military service, which makes sense: the soldier is no foreigner to stress. "During the Civil War for example, palpitations were so common-place that they became known as "soldier's heart".[8] Our Veteran population and their potential exposures and illnesses may lead one to consider the

---

[6] Robinson, (updated July 22, 2013). "Three-Quarters of Your Doctor Bills are Because of This".

[7] Hatz-Seeley, Deborah. March 21, 2014. Chronic stress is linked to the six leading causes of death. Miami Herald in miamiherald.com.

[8] Wallis, Stress: Can We Cope?, Vol. 121 No. 23.

connection between stress and body deterioration. Austrian native doctor Hans Selye also known as the "father of stress research" stated that stress was "the rate of wear and tear in the body". Interesting choice of words. He did not say, wear and tear on the body, rather "in the body".[9] It remains quite interesting how stress may affect the human structure – what is found within the body.

According to the American Institute of Stress (AIS) established in 1978, the word stress is quite difficult to define. AIS states that definitions of stress differ among individuals. "The term 'stress' as it is currently used was coined by Hans Seyle in 1936, who defined it as "the non-specific response of the body to any demand for change".[10] Seyle discovered a relationship between stress and diseases found in animals, as well as in humans. During his experiments, Selye discovered animals subjected to extreme stress displayed negative bodily changes in stomach, adrenals, and lymphoid tissue. Additionally, he stated that persistent stress in animals led to various diseases similar to those found in humans.

The connection with stress and the adrenals is of interest to me. About fifteen years ago, I was under

---

[9] Ibid.

[10] Wallis, Stress: Can We Cope?, Vol. 121 No. 23.

quite a bit of stress while going through a divorce while raising a young child. My daughter was three years old at the time, and the divorce was not amicable. An issue with my back led to imaging, which uncovered an adenoma within my adrenal area. The adrenals are in the endocrine system, and near the kidneys. Actually, we have two adrenal glands, and each sit above the kidneys. The adrenal glands produce hormones such as cortisol and aldosterone.

Aldosterone assists with controlling blood pressure, while cortisol helps regulate stress. An adenoma is a benign tumor, which means it is not cancerous. The discovery of this adrenal gland adenoma led to additional testing and imaging. I recall the endocrinologist telling me that during one certain hormone test, I needed to completely relax and rid myself of any anxiety or stress. I thought to myself, "How can I possibly do this when this is a time of such difficulty in my life?" I was in and out of family court, and my daughter was subjected to much chaos. Then, I was told that I had a medical issue which might warrant surgery. How can one possibly remain calm? I realized then that there had to be a definite connection between life stressors and potential effects on the body – or should I say, *in* the body?

During my research, I also discovered something called adrenal fatigue. Adrenal fatigue is a condition experienced by someone with adrenal issues that is connected to physical and emotional stress. It is when the body is so tired that one may experience symptoms such as body fatigue, aches, pains, and difficulty getting out of bed in the morning. Fortunately, I never experienced adrenal fatigue.

Stressful situations may be subjectively defined as low or high stress. The "fight or flight" analogy correlates with a high stress situation.[11]

Dr. Berczi, a Canadian neuroimmune biologist researcher who studied under Dr. Hans Selye, pointed out that the "fight-or-flight response (also called the fight, flight, freeze, or fawn response [in PTSD], hyperarousal, or the acute stress response) is the physiological reaction that occurs in response to a perceived harmful event, attack, or threat to survival.[12]

Walter Cannon, Harvard professor and physiologist, and Hans Selye originated the term "fight or flight" for an animal's response when threatened.[13] Cannon and Selye connected stress with physiological changes. "Selye showed that when the "fight or flight" response becomes chronic – as it does in battle – long- term chemical changes occur leading to high blood pressure, an increased rate of arteriosclerosis, depression of the

---

[11] Berczi, for Cannoln Walter (1932). Wisdom of the Body.

[12] Ibid.

[13] Wikipedia.org

immune system, and a cascade of other problems."[14] This can then lead to a host of chronic conditions. We are faced with the reality that stress has a negative effect on the body with long-term consequences.

American psychiatrist Thomas Holmes stated that talking about distressing experiences may generate physiological responses. That is why one may experience bodily changes when retelling a story about a stressful or traumatic past experience. Rehashing the experience may bring an individual right back to that moment in time.

Holmes also discovered a connection between tuberculosis patients and life-changing events.

"Stress did not cause the illness, Holmes emphasizes – "It takes a germ" – but tension did seem to promote the disease process."[15]

The 1983 article in Time Magazine, "Stress! Seeking Cures for Modern Anxieties," stated, "In the past 30 years, doctors and health officials have come to realize how heavy a toll stress is taking on the nation's well-being."[16]

Let us take a moment with this. The article, which is over thirty-five years old, states that family practitioners were dealing with stress-related issues dating

---

[14] Wallis, et al, (1983).

[15] Ibid.

[16] Time Magazine's, "Stress! Seeking Cures for Modern Anxieties".

back to the 1950's. So, in present-day, we are now look-ing at 70 years of societal increase in stress tolls. Ac-cording to the American Academy of Family Physi-cians, two-thirds of office visits to family doctors are prompted by stress-related symptoms."[17] The unpre-dictable world we reside in was one cause provided for stress-related symptoms. Stress was a factor for many between the 1950's and 1980's. The National In-stitute of Mental Health reported that in 1985, the per-centage of those eighteen years of age and older with significant stress was 24%, and increased to 35% in 1994.[18] The National Institute of Mental Health also reported that "75% of the general population experi-ences at least 'some stress' every two weeks (National Health Interview Survey 2009) and tranquilizers, an-tidepressants, and anti-anxiety medications account for one-fourth of all prescriptions written in the U.S. each year".[19]

According to the Center for Disease Control and Prevention (CDC) data brief, "Serious Psychological Distress Among Adults: United States, 2009-2013,"

---

[17] Cotton, Stress Management: An Integrated Approach to Therapy, (1990): 3.

[18] Seitz, Operational Definitions for Year 2000 Objectives: Priority Area 6, Mental Health and Mental Disorders, Number 16, February 1998, Center for Disease Control and Prevention.

[19] Freishtat, That Stress-Exercise Connection: How Does This Work?, 2013.

women are more likely than men to have serious psychological distress and among both genders, with an increase in income came a decrease in distress.[20]

We know that stress is problematic; however, stress may also be positive. Stress that moves us forward to get things done and get projects accomplished, may be considered good or healthy stress. If we did not have this, we may remain stagnant without the drive needed to move forward.

Conversely, stress that is problematic and nonproductive is stress that affects our bodies negatively. Overall, we know that acute and chronic stress may wear our bodies down over time and may cause physical effects. Perhaps stress has been with us since the beginning of time. The question is, what can we do about it? Poverty is one such struggle for some, and has existed for many throughout centuries. This may have led to extreme stress and distress. However, generally speaking, life during days past appeared less stressful at times with stable family and home life represented. Is stress a disruptor of harmony? Before we jump to an answer to that question, let's consider stressors that disrupt harmony. On January 23, 2007, the Washington Post indicated in their "Facts on Stress," that money is named the primary factor

---

[20] Weissman, Judith, Ph.D.; et al, 2015.

affecting their stress level in seventy-three percent of Americans.[21]

One may not be able to fix their financial situation during the course of reading this book. However, awareness may lead to a plan of action. One may consider reviewing her/his financial situation and possible strains. It may also be helpful to develop a course of action to decrease financial stress.

Suze Orman, financial guru, provides resources, suggestions, and strategies. In her 2017 blog, "Are You Ready to Declare Your Financial Independence?," she cites a national survey that indicates over fifty percent of employees are stressed about finances.[22] Orman also points out that this was an increase from 2015. While wages may increase annually, perhaps spending does also. This may account for the increase in financial stress among employees. Perhaps working to alleviate debt and increase financial gain can help decrease stress.

An action plan to focus on your financial security may assist with decreasing any stressors associated with it. Also, positive thoughts toward financial success may bring forth change. Another way to battle harmony disruptors is by changing negative thinking,

---

[21] Washington Post, "Facts on Stress," 2007.

[22] Orman, Suze, "Are You Ready to Declare Your Financial Independence"?, 2017.

especially if such thoughts are ongoing. Negative thoughts can be debilitating and lead to more negativity in other aspects of your life. And in turn, this pattern of negative thinking may produce adverse life results.

Positive thinking can certainly combat negativity. When thoughts and words have validating influences, we produce more positive results. Positive affirmations will lead us in a meaningful direction.

Please repeat, I WILL NOT ALLOW STRESS TO DISRUPT MY HARMONY.

Continue to repeat this throughout the day. You may repeat it out loud, or within your mind.

Disharmony may be present in our lives when balance does not exist. Working as a private practice psychotherapist with over two decades of experience, I witnessed the struggles among individuals and have come to realize that none of us are exempt from life's struggles.

Whether rich or poor, Black or White, Hispanic or Asian, gay or straight, young or old, male or female; we all face life's struggles. Unfortunately, some experience more struggles than others. It seems as though one may just come up for air when they're sadly hit again with another stressful event. There are also those experiencing psychiatric illnesses. While some are able to face life's struggles head-on without psychiatric crises, others may not be as fortunate. Individuals may have existing mental health issues.

Psychiatric research paved the way for my understanding of various psychiatric disorders. Early in my career, I was initially hired by an Ivy League university as a research assistant. The research involved studying various psychiatric disorders. I was trained by clinical experts and gained skills in using the *Diagnostic and Statistical Manual of Mental Disorders* (DSM). I enjoyed my work on various psychiatric research studies, but felt a component was missing within the position. While I was able to gather information from individuals, I was unable to process with them what to do about it. I could not assist with putting a clinical plan in place, because I was not a clinician.

This led to my decision to pursue a social work degree. It also paved the way toward clinical endeavors at various hospital emergency rooms and inpatient psychiatric units. My experience has included work with children, adults, couples, families, the elderly, and our military. I witnessed psychosis, suicide attempts, drug and alcohol addiction/withdrawal, homelessness, death, dying, grief, trauma, fear, and loneliness. My clinical work has included experience with victims of domestic violence, sexual assault, and trauma, as well as incarcerated individuals.

Presently, I am employed by a hospital and have had an established private psychotherapy practice for the past decade. I provide counseling to adolescents and adults for an array of issues. My clinical practice focus is cognitive behavioral therapy. Cognitive behavioral therapy is a therapeutic process focused on thoughts and feelings. Clinical sessions include identifying goals and behavior modification. One may seek treatment for help with grieving the loss of a loved one, adjusting to a difficult situation, managing a relationship issue, or handling depression and anxiety – just to name a few.

I may see clients individually, as couples, or with family members. I also specialize in treating trichotillomania – a compulsive disorder where individuals pull their hair out. This disorder is quite interesting because individuals do report stressors, yet most often continue repetitive hair pulling in a relaxed state. Trichotillomania is a repetitive disorder such as skin picking and nail biting. One may ask, how is this a psychiatric disorder? Individuals may have habits like nail biting, playing with hair, and touching one's face. When these behaviors cross over into repetitive behaviors that cause distress and/or interfere with one's functioning, it is no longer just a habit. These disorders also combine factors such as tension, gratification, emotional distress, embarrassment, and shame.

All my training and experience did not quite prepare me for the tragedies of 2001. Following the September 11, 2001 attacks, I traveled to New York City accompanied by my mother, Patricia, a respiratory therapist. Our intentions were to aid victims and their families. Our mission was to assist in any possible way. We were affiliated with the American Red Cross during that time.

Upon our arrival, the New York City streets were silent. We moved by foot, advancing toward lower Manhattan. We worked with police officers and detectives comforting victims' family members entering the Manhattan Armory. The Armory housed military, police, and clinical personnel attempting to unite victims with their loved ones. It was a search and rescue mission at the initial stages during those first days following the attacks.

Families gathered at the Armory in an attempt to obtain possible shreds of information regarding their lost loved ones. Police collected DNA to assist with the search and rescue efforts of missing victims. Mothers, fathers, brothers, husbands, wives, siblings, partners, and friends entered the Armory with hairbrushes, toothbrushes and other items hoping that personal objects would help find those who were missing. Instead, search-and-rescue efforts eventually became recovery with respect to the victims. Shock engulfed the area. Many held on to hope that missing loved ones would be found. Shortly thereafter, their hope turned to dismay. Grief filled the Armory walls; however, sorrow alone did not exist in that building. Love was there, as well as strangers surrounding each other and there was an overwhelming connection. We were all one people, one country: the United States of America. Celebrities were among the volunteers; yet egos found no place inside the building. The Star-Spangled Banner played throughout the structure, which housed tables of donated food for families and workers. Bonding, true caring, and empathy existed. Time has passed and perhaps "time heals" – or does it? The news changes daily and has become background noise as we move forward in our lives. We seldom discuss the 9/11 tragedies; however, most know exactly where they were on that beautiful sunny September morning. Our hectic days continue as the seasons change.

Perhaps this is constructive as time passing allows us to return to a certain normalcy in our everyday lives. Our "normal" daily stressors may return. However, daily stressors that are excessive and chronic may lead to additional mental health issues.

According to Daniel K. Hall-Flavin, M.D. a Mayo Clinic Psychiatrist, "persistent or chronic stress has the potential to put vulnerable individuals at a substantially increased risk of depression, anxiety, and many other emotional difficulties."[23] Scientists have noted that changes in brain function – in the areas of the hypothalamus and the pituitary gland – may play a key role in stress – induced emotional problems."[24]

Our present-day reality is becoming more and more corrupted by chronic stress. Sadly, we are faced with devastating events which include terror attacks throughout our world. Whether it be a school, mall, nightclub, movie theater, cafe, or festive gathering, we are all affected by the inexcusable horrors. The reality is that during daily living moments, one may face a senseless death. This is our 21st century reality. The unknown can be overwhelming for some. Chronic stress may lead to anxiety and/or depression for individuals. Symptoms may interfere with peace of mind. Some may feel paralyzed by fear and left feeling helpless. It may be difficult for one to consider solutions or other coping mechanisms. It is important to reach out for help if you are feeling helpless and/or hopeless.

---

[23] Daniel K. Hall-Flavin, M.D.

[24] Mayo Clinic.com 2/25/2010 Stress Management Can Chronic Stress Cause Depression?.

Coexisting disorders may also contribute to substance abuse or dependence issues with those suffering from its effects. Such individuals may self-medicate to relieve depressive or nervous symptoms. According to the *Diagnostic and Statistical Manual of Mental Disorders*, Fourth Edition, Generalized Anxiety Disorder is excessive worry for more days than not about a number of concerns.[25] This lasts over a period of at least six months and the individual experiences specific symptoms associated with anxiety. It is important that a medical diagnosis be ruled out prior to being labeled a psychiatric disorder.

The anxiety related symptoms must not alone be associated with a coexisting disorder such as Obsessive-Compulsive Disorder, Panic Disorder, or a Substance Disorder. Rather, the worries for the individual are difficult to control and may cause physical symptoms. In turn, this may contribute to impairment or significant distress in one's occupational, social, or another important area of functioning. A person with Generalized Anxiety Disorder may experience restlessness, fatigue, irritability, muscle tension, sleep disturbance and difficulty concentrating. He or she will find it difficult to stop worrying, and the worries are about a number of issues. An individual experiencing anxiety

---

[25] Diagnostic and Statistical Manual of Mental Disorders, Fourth Edition, Generalized Anxiety Disorder.

may find it difficult to function as he/she once did previously. Nervousness may interfere with normal daily life and lead to clinical attention being sought.

It is important that a professional diagnose symptoms. Self-diagnosis may lead to increased unwarranted concerns and worry. There are specifics that a professional will evaluate, which the average individual may not. The information found in this book is for reference purposes only. If a reader feels the need to self-diagnose a clinical disorder, it is important that he/she consult with a professional clinician. Employee assistance programs, insurance companies, and local mental health agencies may assist with psychotherapy referrals in your area. If an individual is suicidal or homicidal, she or he should call 911 or go to their nearest emergency room.

Personal experiences and those of others appear throughout this book. All names and situations have been changed, as well as any identifiable information, for privacy and confidentiality purposes. Disruptors of harmony may be subjective. What you believe disrupts your harmony, may not be what I believe disrupts my harmony. However, throughout my own experiences, those encountered in my life, as well as within my clinical practice, I have established a list of harmony disruptors. You may add to this list if you see fit. You may visit WWW.ALEGEEMPOWER.COM to discover new ways to combat harmony disruptors in your life and express yours as well.

Please feel free to add a positive quote or sentiment there. This book includes inspirational and positive quotations for a reason, and I believe it is important to insert background information about individuals quoted for a better understanding of who they are, what may have contributed to their particular stressors, and how they overcame the challenges. We may recall quotes of well-known individuals but seldom can explain their history and accomplishments.

The individuals I have chosen for quotations may have also experienced adversities which they attempted to overcome in their own lives. These individuals are not claimed to be superior to others in any way, but rather inspirational in their own ways. You may have many more inspirational individuals in your life, which could certainly be included. It is important to keep those positive connections in your life. Make mention of those who are inspirational and provide positive influences. It is also important to recognize what disrupts your harmony. Who or what are those culprits?

Please repeat, I WILL NOT ALLOW STRESS TO DISRUPT MY HARMONY.

Chapter Two
Terror

"TERROR - A state of intense or overwhelming fear"[26]

The only devils in the world are those running around in our hearts - that is where the battle should be fought.[27]

—Mahatma Gandhi

Mahatma Gandhi (1869 – 1948) was a major political and spiritual leader of India and the Indian independence movement. He was the pioneer of Satyagraha — resistance to tyranny through mass civil disobedience, firmly

---

[26] Merriam-Webster.Com Dictionary

[27] Motivationmentalist.com, Chris Tan, 17 March 2015. Mahatma Gandhi-Inspirational Quotes, Films, and Speech.

founded upon ahimsa or total non-violence—which led India to independence and inspired movements for civil rights and freedom across the world. Gandhi practiced non-violence and truth in all situations, and advocated that others do the same. He lived modestly in a self-sufficient residential community while wearing the traditional Indian dhoti and shawl, woven with yarn he had hand spun on a charkha. He ate simple vegetarian food but also undertook long fasts as means of both self-purification and social protest.[28]

Terror, a disruptor of harmony is contrary to what Gandhi promoted. A terrorist is one who works against the freedoms of others. The Federal Emergency Management Agency (FEMA) defines terrorism as "the use of force or violence against persons or property in violation of the criminal laws of the United States for purposes of intimidation, coercion, or ransom. FEMA adds that terrorism includes terrorist threats, as well as causes of intense fear with people."[29]

The United States of America is built on freedom of life, liberty, and the pursuit of happiness. Our founding fathers declared that the United States people be protected with equality for all.

---

[28] Wikipedia, Mahatma Gandhi.
[29] Fema.gov, 4.1 General Information about Terrorism, page 148.

The Merriam-Webster Collegiate Dictionary, Tenth Edition, defines the following:

Life, "the period from birth to death..."

Liberty, "1: the quality or state of being free:
a: the power to do as one pleases
b: freedom from physical restraint..."

Happiness, "a state of well-being and contentment"[30]

A terrorist often wishes to destroy the rights of others. Therefore, stripping happiness from one's life. "The Giver of life gave it for happiness and not for the wretchedness."

-Thomas Jefferson to
James Monroe, 1782.[31]

According to the Department of Justice Federal Bureau of Investigations, "A hate crime, also known as a bias crime," is a criminal offense committed against a person, property, or society that is motivated, in whole or in part, by the offender's bias

---

[30] The Merriam-Webster Collegiate Dictionary, Tenth Edition.
[31] ME 4:196, Papers 6:186, (Jefferson on Politics & Government: Inalienable Rights)

against a race, religion, disability, sexual orientation, or ethnicity/national origin. Since 1990, the Department of Justice continues to collect data on hate crimes throughout the United States. In the year 2006, 2,105 law enforcement agencies reported 7,722 hate crime incidents involving 9,080 offenses (Department of Justice, Federal Bureau of Investigations).[32]

Following national concern over bias-motivated crimes, Congress enacted the Hate Crimes Prevention Act and the Hate Crime Statistics Act of 1990. The attack on and death of Matthew Shepard, a gay college student, brought enhancements to the Federal hate crime law.[33]

Many years have passed since Shepard's 1998 brutal beating and crucifixion. A federal bill to expand hate-crimes protection to protect women is the Violence Against Women Reauthorization Act of 2013. The law provides some additional support and resources.[34] We may have progressed in some ways but still have further to go with equality. There remain no laws specifically protecting the transsexual community. Perhaps we will see change in the near future.

---

[32] Department of Justice, Federal Bureau of Investigations

[33] Religioustolerance.org

[34] U.S. Department of Health & Human Services, Office on Women's Health. Laws on violence against women March 02, 2018.

The terrorist attacks of September 11, 2001 shocked our nation when religious fanatics disturbed the inalienable rights of others. Terrorists murdered 2,973 human lives within the United States of America. Many individuals were at work at the time of the attacks.

However, the terrorists never stripped our spirits. We united as a country to help those in need. Workers came from across the United States to support one another. Our courage grew as we stood as one nation. We could have crumbled and remained paralyzed, but instead, we became stronger in numbers. All must remember that when adversity strikes, we have a choice. We may choose to lay down, or stand up. Standing for one's beliefs may mean different things to people. It may simply mean to express and embrace those beliefs.

Confucius said, "Before you embark on a journey of revenge, dig two graves".[35]

While we have discussed the formal definition of terrorism, terror comes in many forms. Terror may be inside or outside our homes. Fear and terror go hand and hand. Within an abusive relationship, one may experience terror. Physical and emotional abusers instill fear within their victims. Manipulation and control threaten the individual, and this may lead to fear and

---

[35] Goodreads, Confucius

helplessness. The loss of freedom a victim experiences may be emotional terrorism. Self-esteem is often lowered due to criticism and loss of control. Fear of the unknown weighs on the victim's mind. An individual may fixate on the abuser or terrorist's next strike. The question then becomes, how does one combat the terrorist? Whether it be emotional, verbal, or physical abuse, one must first recognize it. Instead of berating yourself and fixating on what you are not doing or doing wrong, think about all the things you are doing right.

Consider your good qualities as a human being, parent, daughter, son, sibling, or friend. Tell yourself that you are worthy of a good life and a peaceful existence. Contemplate a plan of action for how you will change your life in a positive direction. Visualize what that life will look like. Mental imagery is a very good tool. Imagine yourself in a peaceful place and life. How will you be different? Close your eyes at night and awaken each morning with a positive statement. Believe that you are capable of changing your life and not allowing another to control you in any way.

Terrorism may strip another of freedom, peace, and tranquility. Malcom X once said, "You can't separate peace from freedom because no one can be at peace unless he has his freedom"[36]

---

[36] Hunch.com

Malcom X was born Malcom Little in 1925 and was one of eight children. His mother was a homemaker, and his father was a Baptist minister and civil rights activist. During the latter part of the 1920's, their home was burned to the ground. A few years later, Malcolm's dad was found dead on the trolley tracks, and many people believed it was murder. Malcolm's mother later became institutionalized with emotional issues, while Malcolm and his siblings were separated and transported to various foster homes and orphanages.[37]

According to Malcolm X's history, he dreamed of becoming a lawyer, and was a very good student with excellent grades. One day his dreams were shattered when a teacher told him that being a lawyer was out of the question, and "no realistic goal for a n...."[38] He eventually partook in criminal activities, which led to a prison sentence. During his imprisonment, Malcolm studied the Muslim religion.

Following his release from prison, Malcolm became a minister and spokesperson for the Nation of Islam. When he later discovered that his mentor, the religious leader Elijah Muhammad, was unfaithful to the Muslim religious teachings by having many affairs as well as children, Malcolm experienced a

---

[37] Malcolmx.com
[38] Ibid.

damaging jolt. He was faithful to his beliefs, and the shattering news led to his disaffiliation with the Nation of Islam. This led Malcolm to form his own religious association – the Muslim Mosque, Inc. Malcolm X was gunned down at the age of thirty-nine during a New York speaking engagement in 1965. His wife was pregnant with their twin daughters at the time.[39]

There are other activists such as Malcolm X who worked to fight against social injustice, fear, and terror among individuals. Pearl S. Buck was an American born writer and Pulitzer Prize winner of *The Good Earth* in the 1930's. She spent most of her life residing in China. She adopted several children, and later moved back to the United States. Buck was a civil rights and women's rights activist. She established the first interracial, international adoption agency in 1949. It outraged her that interracial and Asian children were considered unadoptable. The Pearl S. Buck Foundation in Green Hills Farm, New Jersey continues on with Pearl Buck's legacy and dream. Pearl S. Buck once said, "None who have always been free can understand the terrible fascinating power of the hope of freedom to those who are not free."[40] Pearl S. Buck lived her life helping others. She understood that certain racial and ethnic distinctions made a difference

---

[39] Ibid

[40] Quotes.liberty-tree.ca

in the adoption process. She witnessed how some children were oppressed while awaiting a family to call their own. They lacked the same freedom and equal right to adoption as others.

"Everything that is really great and inspiring is created by the individual who can labor in freedom," Albert Einstein.[41] According to nobelprize.org, Albert Einstein (1879-1955), although born in Germany, later renounced his citizenship due to political differences. He became a United States citizen and professor until his retirement. Following World War II, Albert Einstein was offered the Presidency of Israel. Although he declined the offer, he was instrumental in establishing the Hebrew University of Jerusalem.[42]

Please repeat, I WILL NOT ALLOW TERROR OR FEAR TO DISRUPT MY HARMONY.

If you find yourself in a state of fear of another individual, please seek guidance and assistance within your community. If the fear involves intimate partner or domestic violence, there are agencies throughout the United States to assist. The National Domestic Violence Hotline is 1-800-799-7233 or TTY 1-800-787-3224. The National Crime Victim Hotline is

---

[41] Quotation.cloud
[42] Prize.org

1- 855-4-VICTIM (1-855-484-2846). If you are in imminent danger, please dial 911.

Chapter Three
Deceit

"DECEIT - The act or practice of deceiving; conceal-ment or distortion of the truth for the purpose of misleading; duplicity; fraud; cheating."[43]

I recall my brother, Joe, sharing a story many years ago. He was not particularly fond of his company's secretary. Frustrated with her during a call one day while he was hanging up the telephone, he made a negative comment about her. To his surprise, the tel-ephone call had not yet disconnected, and she over-heard him. Later that day, Joe received a call from his boss. He relayed the following words, "Character is when no one is watching". Character is something that is developed over time. Positive character traits

---

[43] Dictionary.com

are principles to live by and may include qualities such as honesty, thoughtfulness, and respect.

Deceit is certainly a character flaw.

"The circumstances where you live determine your reputation, while the truth you believe determines your character.

Reputation is what you are supposed to be; character is what you are. Reputation is the photograph; character is the face.

Reputation comes over one from without; character grows up from within.

Reputation is what you have when you come to a new community; character is what you have when you go away.

Your reputation is learned in an hour; your character does not come to light for a year. Reputation is made in a moment; character is built in a lifetime.

Reputation grows like a mushroom; character grows like the oak.

A single newspaper report gives you your reputation; a life of toil gives you your character.

Reputation makes you rich or makes you poor; character makes you happy or makes you miserable.

Reputation is what men say about you on your tombstone; character is what angels say about you before the throne of God."

-William Hersey Davis[44]

William Hersey Davis was born in 1887, and died in 1950. He was a professor at the Southern Baptist Theological Seminary. William Hersey Davis was a scholar with medals and honors.

When you are faced with someone who is deceitful, the impact may make it difficult for future engagement. It is even more difficult when it is unexpected from a close friend or loved one. Deception will lead to increased stress in your life whether you are the one who is deceived or you are the one being deceptive. Unless an individual is remorseful and willing to change her/his behavior, it is almost impossible to continue the relationship and expect that it will not affect you in some way. Continued toleration of lies and deceit of another will most likely have an impact on your self-esteem. Negative consequences will ensue.

There are varying degrees of dishonesty, which may play a part in one's decision to keep or abandon a relationship with a dishonest person. When

---

[44] Goodreads

dishonesty and deception continue over time, you may be facing a true phony. A phony is an imposter – one who misleads others by fake appearances. Such an individual is not genuine, but rather fraudulent in essence. I am sure we may all recall a time in life when we were dishonest in some way, or the first encounter we had with another person who was dishonest.

I recall my first encounter with dishonesty and although it was not a deep hurt, it was memorable. It does however indicate to me that at any age, if a friend or loved one is dishonest, it may be something you do not forget. Depending on what it is, it may or may not have a significant impact. It appears to depend upon the circumstances surrounding it.

In my experience, I was about nine years old at the time. Elvis Presley was in town, and I was about to attend his performance with my mother. My childhood friend reported that she was going to the show as well. She concocted an elaborate plan for us to meet during intermission at the venue. It was not until the day of the performance that I discovered otherwise. My friend informed me that she never had any intention of attending the show. It was all just a joke, and the joke was on me. I was looking forward to our meeting and the excitement of the concert. I am sure she meant no harm by this, and probably even thought it was quite funny.

While I felt badly at the time, we remained friends through the years. We laugh about this to this day as it was an innocent prank. She remains my dearest and oldest friend. One may receive details and later discover those details are lies. The picture shared by another may not be true. In other instances, a partner may discover a loved one's emails to a co-worker that may not necessarily be innocent or work related. Instead, some individuals may find inappropriate content. One may be shocked to learn his/her spouse is engaged in sexual chat rooms.

Immediate gratification is often at the expense of relationships. Some couples struggle financially to make ends meet when suddenly a spouse may discover savings being spent on Internet sex sites. When a partner or spouse is deceitful, it may ruin the relationship beyond repair. Once betrayed, it may be difficult to trust again. This may lead an individual to react in ways they never thought they would.

One may find oneself operating as a detective. Many begin checking on their partner/spouse, searching for possible clues along the way. Sometimes guilt may even set in when the partner is no longer trusted, yet continues to plead his/her case as a victim. After time passes and personal investigations perhaps produce little evidence, one may stop further searches.

However, that does not mean all is forgotten. Thoughts of being deceived and other potential lies may consume a person. After all, nobody wants to feel like a fool. If there was something to discover, wouldn't you want to uncover the evidence? Some, with the monetary means, may go as far as hiring a private investigator. As time passes, feelings may settle and one may be able to trust again. You may even feel slight guilt about your mistrust. You may question yourself, "Was I too demanding and my expectations too high?" You may find yourself making excuses like, he/she is introverted, works so much, and/or has so few friends.

For some, friendship interactions are mainly via the Internet. Some are able to shed their social skin via the computer only. This may be very concerning and dangerous for a partner. The question is, should one pay more attention to one's gut instincts? Do some just make excuses for a partner/spouse? If you find hidden information about your spouse that crosses the line in some way, your gut instinct may be true. Your inner self may be telling you something.

When this leads you to completing detective work on your spouse, you may begin to ask yourself how your time may be better spent. Should your energy be spent elsewhere?

Afterall, life is really short. When we recall the tragedies of 9/11 and those that have occurred since, including Sandy Hook, you must keep in perspective your health and that of your child/children. If you have a job, a roof over your head, love, a healthy family, and friends; you have everything! If you do not, be grateful for what positives you do have in your life.

You may not have many friends, but you have one you can trust. You may not have a huge family, but a loving sibling. This is all you really need. And if you do not have any family and friends, go out and start meeting new people. It is never too late to engage new relationships. You may consider volunteer work or a meetup with an interest group. If you cannot find a group you want, start your own! There are options and many things you may consider. Go out there and make your impact on this world!

Begin a daily journal about what you are grateful for. Keep in perspective how your life may have been pulled into pointless chaos. Consider what and how you give of yourself and how others should reciprocate. If you are faithful, you should expect faithfulness in return. If you are kind, you should expect that same kindness to you. You deserve that!

When one discovers a partner may be unfaithful, it is important to communicate and learn about the actual truth. Stories may or may not be lies and/or exaggerated. Sometimes things may look a certain way, but in reality they are quite different. Maybe couple's counseling is an option. If infidelity is the circumstance, it may feel gut wrenching, but counseling may help. It may lead you to a search for the truth. One may feel repulsed by the thought that a spouse is unfaithful, but feel the need to search for clues.

You may discover buried secrets deep beneath the ocean's surface. You may find an imposter. You may discover issues that you never knew about your partner, and uncover deeper roots. We all have our own styles of communication.

Some couples may have limited discussions. I like to call it, "surface talk". They skim the surface and seldom get deep within conversation. Deep conversation means fully expressing one's feelings, answering questions a partner asks, and divulging unpleasantries of one's past. Some individuals talk, talk, talk – but the content lacks substance. They have difficulties speaking about emotions and experiences, which may be unpleasant. They may barely scratch the surface and their dialogue may lack real exchanges about life's desires or feelings. Some lead lives of facade with distorted truths. You or your partner may have an artificial view of yourself and the world around you. If one is truly remorseful, it will take hard work on both sides to mend the relationship. You may need marriage therapy or spiritual/religious guidance. With time, you may rebuild a healthy relationship.

It may never return to what it once was. It may be a new and improved partnership. There were issues in the old relationship and therefore – you would not want to return to what it once was.

If the relationship is not worth salvaging and the cheating spouse is not remorseful, it will probably happen again. As a clinician, I have heard both sides. In some cases, the unfaithful spouse expects the partner to "get over it" fairly quickly. They really do not want to keep discussing it. They want to forget about it and put it behind them. Perhaps they are struggling with feelings of guilt.

What one must realize is there is no special time clock or a miracle wand to have that individual forget the actions and not feel the pain. One must be patient with their partner and allow healing. The partner who experienced the hurt may benefit from individual counseling as well. Actually, each may benefit from individual, as well as couple's counseling. It is acceptable with most insurances to allow for both. If, however, couples are not remorseful and willing to do the work, they may wish to end the relationship. You may spend precious years trying to fix a problem your partner does not understand and/or care to mend. If the individual is truly deceitful in other ways as well, this may become evident. Rid yourself of the deceitful individuals in your life. They will cause increased stress and eventually deteriorate your health.

Individuals must decide what is best for them. When is enough, enough? If you are consumed with mistrusting another, it may be best to let go of the relationship and keep hold of your sanity. Seeking some professional help and guidance from an unbiased clinician may help sort through such difficulties. One may reach out to a social worker or psychologist in your area. Your healthcare insurance company can provide you with information about local therapists. If you are without insurance, please check with your local community counseling agencies. One may even wish to seek guidance from the clergy, as clinical and spiritual guidance may be most helpful.

A man who lies to himself, and believes his own lies, becomes unable to recognize the truth – either in himself or in anyone else, and he ends up losing respect for himself and for others.

When he has no respect for anyone, he can no longer love, and in him, he yields to his impulses, indulges in the lowest form of pleasure, and behaves in the end like an animal in satisfying his vices. And it all comes from lying to others and to yourself.

-Fyodor Dostoyevsky[45]

Fyodor Dostoyevsky (1821-1881) was a Russian born author of *Crime and Punishment* and other books. His early home life was troubled with an oppressive father. His writings were said to shed light on social awareness. He wrote about life struggles and redemption through suffering.

Please repeat, I WILL NOT ALLOW DECEIT TO DISRUPT MY HARMONY.

---

[45] Quotes.liberty-tree.ca

Chapter Four
Imbalance

"Imbalance - The state or condition of lacking balance"[46]

America's future will be determined by the home and the school. The child becomes largely what he is taught; hence we must watch what we teach, and how we live.

> -Jane Addams
> (September 6, 1860 –
> May 21, 1935)[47]

Jane Addams received the first-ever awarded honorary degree to a female by Yale University in 1910. She wrote *Peace and Bread in Time of War*

---

[46] Dictionary.com
[47] Brainyquote.com

for which she won the Nobel Peace Prize. However, this victory did not come without its own struggles. Jane had spinal issues as a child, but was later a pioneer social worker who opened the Hull House for the underprivileged in Chicago.

Imbalance may come in different forms in our lives. A state of disequilibrium may come in the form of bad habits, greed, hatred, ill-faith, weight fluctuations, emotional instability, physical health deteriorations, or self-image stressors. Such imbalances may lead to self-medicating with food, substances, gambling, and other dysfunctional addictions. An example would be substance abuse or dependence. An individual may abuse alcohol or drugs to block difficult thoughts or feelings. The imbalance may be a result of the substance or the substance may be attempting to mask an already existent imbalance. Substance abuse is determined when an individual has significant impairment or distress over a one-year period of time. One may continue substance use despite difficulties fulfilling major obligations within their homes, school, or work environments. He/she may continue use despite interpersonal or social interference, and there may be legal complications involved with use.

This diagnosis may also include an individual continuing to use despite hazardous consequences, such as driving while intoxicated. Substance dependence, on the other hand, includes criteria such as developed tolerance – when an individual may need increased amounts of the substance to achieve their desired effects. Additionally, withdrawal symptoms may occur from discontinuation of the substance.

Such symptoms when pertaining to alcohol abstinence for example may include: shakiness, nausea/vomiting, seizures, and stomach pains. People with substance dependence patterns usually spend a great deal of their time using or recovering from a substance's effects. Consequently, important responsibilities are given up as a result.

Our minds and bodies need to exist in a state of equilibrium. When our bodies are taxed, it is common for our minds to be affected, and vice versa. To live in total balance may be an unrealistic expectation. However, there are certain cultures who may be better at successfully achieving such goals. The Buddhist Masters of Tibet appear to have achieved balance of mind and body in their lives. According to the "Eight Steps to Happiness, the Buddhist Way of Loving Kindness,"

> Happiness is a state of mind, so the real source of happiness must lie within the mind, not in external conditions. If our mind is pure and peaceful we shall be happy, regardless of

our external circumstances, but if it is impure and unpeaceful we can never be truly happy, no matter how hard we try to change our external conditions. We could change our home or our partner countless times, but until we change our restless, discontented mind we shall never find true happiness.[48]

According to religioustolerance.org, Buddhism is the fourth largest religion in the world.

In 535 B.C., Siddhartha Gautama founded Buddhism in India. As a prince, he left his royalty to become a monk and achieve enlightenment aside from materialism. Buddhism expanded across Asia, and now exists in its newest form called Modern Buddhism.

"Buddha believed that we are temporal creations born to lives of sorrow and suffering. This suffering is a result of selfish desires that chain people to the wheel of insubstantial impermanent things.[49] Buddhists live their lives according to Dharma – the law and nature of being or existence.

Atisha, a renowned Buddhist, stated,

---

[48] Eight Steps to Happiness: The Buddhist Way of Loving Kindness, Pages 3-4. Kelsang Gyatso

[49] Contenderminitries.com

The greatest achievement is selflessness.
The greatest worth is self-mastery.
The greatest quality is seeking to serve
others.
The greatest precept is continual awareness.
The greatest medicine is the emptiness of
everything.
The greatest action is not conforming
with the world's ways. The greatest
magic is transmuting the passions.
The greatest generosity is non-attach-
ment. The greatest goodness is a
peaceful mind. The greatest patience
is humility.
The greatest effort is not concerned with
results. The greatest meditation is a
mind that lets go.
The greatest wisdom is seeing through
appearances.[50]

Each person's story is the unique indicator of his or her life. Our lives are but many stories entwined over time. Thankfully, our existences are not representative of one story alone, but rather various stories throughout our lifespans.

---

[50] Religioustolerance.com

This brings to mind the recent tragedy of a man in his latter twenties. For the purposes of this book, I will name him John and his fiancé, Lori. John was engaged to be married following a one-year courtship. The girl he chose to marry appeared quite kind and pleasant on the surface. They seldom argued, and outwardly appeared very compatible. What was discovered over time was Lori's secretive and dark nature. Lori did appear to have some insecurities, such as jealousy.

These insecurities grew over time and reached a point of causing difficulties within their relationship. Lori needed increased amounts of reassurance and attention. Her tearfulness and manifested issues often led to frustrations with her fiancé, John. Lori's insecurities impacted and limited her life's ambitions. She was paralyzed to the point of having difficulties sustaining employment, and with that came an inability to attain future goals. She often apologized for her behavior when she realized that her accusations were without merit. She stated that it was immaturity and insecurity due to her negative past relationships. Lori did not appear to be harsh or mean spirited in any way; she was just insecure and immature.

We all are filled with imperfections. However, the imperfections crossed the line for John, which caused the demise of their relationship. The true core of an individual may be fractured, and in time, become more evident to others. A vile core may drain the individual and create a greater disequilibrium than may have already existed. This young woman in particular was actually driven by materialism and in great competition with her younger sibling. The reasons behind this are unknown, but the sibling rivalry did present. Lori reported frustrations that her younger sister married before her. The details of Lori's wedding plans mimicked those of her younger sister. These included the same posh seaside venue, caterer, and music among others.

An individual's foundation may be strong with solid ground, or cracked – causing deterioration over time. Some may be unaware of this, while others may recognize it but choose to dismiss it. The imbalance of an individual does not necessarily reflect their character. One may make decisions which are out of character during different stages of one's life. True character is displayed within time. One may conceal this, but it cannot be hidden forever. Abraham Lincoln once said:

You can fool some of the people all of the time, and all of the people some of the time, but you cannot fool all of the people all of the time.[51]

Abraham Lincoln, the 16th president of the United States, was born in 1809 and raised on a Kentucky farm. President Lincoln opposed slavery and brought the country through the Civil War. On Good Friday, April 14, 1865, President Abraham Lincoln was assassinated at Ford's Theatre in Washington by John Wilkes Booth, an actor.

When I speak about an individual's foundation, I do not mean that one with a strong character will not experience imbalance. Imbalance may be the result of many factors and experiences – many of which may be out of the control of the person. However, the following is an example of an individual's imbalance that led to emotional ill-being.

During the midst of their one-year courtship, John and Lori became engaged. They planned an elaborate wedding for the following year, which would be attended by both family and friends. They traveled and experienced life to the fullest – or so it appeared. They presented as excited about their wedding plans and future lives together, and this couple was financially

---

[51] Quoteland.com

secure due to John's business and entrepreneurial adventures.

John and Lori discovered that she was pregnant just shy of the second year of their relationship. Following family pressures, a decision was made at that time to have a much smaller wedding with immediate family only. Lori did not voice any concerns about this, but rather remained quiet. It became evident within a short period of time that her disappointment was more about her desire for a large traditional wedding – the same type of wedding that her sister once had. There appeared to be competition and jealousy between the two young women. John began planning a small wedding, while Lori remained disinterested and indifferent. She never voiced any concerns or indicated issues about a smaller wedding, however her demeanor continued to deteriorate over time as she became irritable and withdrawn.

She appeared to go along with John, but held secret plans of her own. The elaborate wedding she envisioned led her to secure a venue space for the following year. She did not share this information with John or her family. She began voicing concerns to John about her probability of miscarriage due to family history. This was unusual, since no physician presented cause for concern. She also made this information known to others about the potential like-lihood of miscarriage, as if she was preparing them for the inevitable. Family and friends expressed that they found it odd for someone to speak about this in such a way. This brought about suspicion. Some be-lieved that Lori was setting a future scene. Quickly, Lori began stating that she was having medical com-plications, yet made little attempt to be examined by a physician. She was passive and nonchalant about her medical concerns.

John encouraged Lori to see a physician. Follow-ing a telephone conversation when Lori mentioned matter-of-factly that she was probably losing the preg-nancy, John demanded that she be seen profession-ally. Lori again resisted, but John would not allow it to continue and accompanied her to be examined by a physician. The examination concluded a stable preg-nancy and healthy baby. Lori cried throughout the en-tire examination, and would not make eye contact with the doctor or John.

Lori continued with the same irrational behavior over the next week. Late one evening, Lori contacted John stating that she lost the baby and was returning home from the hospital. She never called John to ac-company her to the hospital, and appeared unemo-tional about her loss. Instead, she was defensive about her predisposition to miscarriages, stating family members had experienced them previously. She expressed to John earlier that day that they would make wonderful parents.

John, knowing the truth in his heart, ended their relationship. Lori made numerous attempts to reconcile, but to no avail. She denied an abortion until months later when her life appeared to be spiraling out of control. Lori was seen intoxicated at local bars displaying outbursts and advances toward different men. She admitted to John that her life was out of control, and she was in need of medication. Lori confessed months later that she had aborted their child. The question in John's mind was whether the child was really his child. Lori's paranoia, accusations about unfaithfulness, and insecurities may have actually been a deflection of her own lies and deceptions. Lori may or may not find balance in her life. Only her future will tell.

Some say that Saint Rose of Lima is the patron saint of the unborn child. Saint Rose of Lima was born in Lima, Peru as Isabel in 1586 and died in 1617. Saint Rose stated,

Let all men know that grace comes after tribulation. Let them know that without the burden of afflictions it is impossible to reach the height of grace. Let them know that the

gifts of grace increase as the struggles increase. Let men take care not to stray and be deceived. This is the only true stairway to paradise, and without the cross they can find no road to climb to heaven.[52]

Often balance and happiness co-exist. Individuals may define happiness differently. One may believe that wealth will bring happiness, only to discover that they are disillusioned by its empty promises. Often, our society has educated us to believe that love is our goal in life. Marriage and family is often the cornerstone of our livelihoods. Each person has expectations about his or her life. We may be disillusioned by marriage, unaware of its many aspects.

Perhaps classes about marriage and family should be more embedded into the curriculum throughout our school years. The realistic components of married life should be included among subjects like math, reading, and writing. Additionally, while it is important that our children grow up to be independent and productive members of society, it is just as important that we not raise materialistic and greedy human beings. Perhaps volunteer work should also be a major aspect of our education. Many adults

---

[52] www.catholic -forum.com

who rid themselves of material possessions or give back with volunteer work may find balance.

Money does not make the individual. It can assist in limiting many stressors for those who are struggling to survive financially though. Additionally, money for some, may add additional stressors. This can connect with greed or the added responsibilities that may come about. An example of this would be more financial security with a business that now employs more workers. The business owner may be consumed with responsibilities and pressures of employees. Money does not define who we truly are, although we live in a world measured by economic status. Self-evaluate any negatives like greediness, hatred, ill faith, hopelessness, or poor self-image. Write down the items you wish to change, and set some realistic goal dates. Try working on one at a time. If ill faith is one such goal, and it is too difficult for you to walk into a place of worship, you may start with your own spirituality.

Think about a time in your life when your spirituality was different. Consider meditating, and being grateful to a higher being. Meditation can be a great way of relieving anxiety and bringing balance to your life. Let loved ones know that you need some time for yourself. Find a quiet place where you can sit on the floor with your legs crossed. Gather some comfortable meditation pillows for yourself to encourage sitting upright and prop the pillows beneath you and behind your back. Dim the lights to create a peaceful and relaxing atmosphere. Create an image in your mind, really study the scenery and its details.

Many individuals find the ocean a tranquil scene. You may want to picture yourself sitting alone on a beach with the sun's warmth on your body. Picture the various ocean colors. Imagine yourself feeling the waves' movements. Grant yourself enough time to settle into the scene. Allow your mind to visualize the waves traveling in towards the shore and out to sea. Any thoughts or worries can be placed on the waves as they move through the ocean. If this visualization is too difficult, picture a piece of sea glass at the edge of the shore. Study its colors and notice how the sun shines upon it. Watch it carefully as the waves crash at the shoreline and move across the piece of glass. This will take practice, but it is well worth it.

Marsha Linehan is a clinician who writes about Mindfulness and Radical Acceptance. Radical acceptance is a practice of acceptance. It is accepting your life where it is in the present moment completely. This does not mean you deny any difficulties or struggles, but rather embrace them in the present moment.

An example of this may be grief. One may be experiencing extreme sadness with the loss of a loved one - there is no denying this. A deep emptiness one may feel following the loss of a loved one is grief. However, during the mindful meditation exercise, one can let go completely, freeing the mind with acceptance.

Accepting where your life is within that moment of hurt and sadness is key. A mindful meditative exercise described by Marsha Linehan in her book, *Skills Training Manual for Treating Borderline Personality Disorder, First Ed/Edition 1* is for any and all individuals. One does not need a mental health diagnosis to partake in meditation. Consider a warm autumn day with a tree and a stream below.[53] Study the tree in your mind, and focus on one particular leaf.

Create that leaf with various colors and evaluate its shape. Pay attention to the leaf's markings, and see how its stem connects to the tree. As a soft breeze blows the leaf from the tree into the stream below, imagine the leaf slowly floating across the water. Any anxieties or worries you may have should be placed on the leaf as it glides through the stream. Continue this for at least fifteen minutes. Try not to get discouraged if you find you are having a difficult time staying in the moment. Realize that you will be distracted by sounds and even silence. Acknowledge the distractions, and then return your focus to the leaf. Practice

---

[53] Linehan, Skills Training Manual for Treating Borderline Personality Disorder, First Ed/Edition 1, 1993.

this daily – either before bedtime or first thing in the morning. Be in the moment as much as you possibly can. If worries enter your mind, acknowledge them, and place the worries on the leaf. Watch the leaf float away. You can address your concerns or chores once you have completed your meditation.

Another exercise that Marsha Linehan discusses is a breathing exercise. As you inhale, you may repeat, "May I accept things as they are," and as you exhale you say, "May I enjoy serenity and peace." Continue this for at least fifteen minutes each day during meditation time. I enjoy switching my meditation practices. At times, I may practice visualization and at other times, breathing. Years ago, I found it difficult to use breathing as a meditation. I found that concentrating too much on my breathing led to rapid respirations. This had an opposite effect for what I was trying to achieve; I was becoming more anxious. What I did that worked was stop the breathing meditation, in favor of more visualization. Overtime, I eased my way into breathing meditation. I now switch back and forth with these practices easily.

Such skills would be beneficial to all. Training children at young ages to find peace and tranquility within can truly shape their futures. Capturing the child's freedom of experience, which is often lost with aging, would be a powerful tool into adulthood.

Children often play carefree and unbothered – how wonderful if we as adults could feel that sensation of freedom again.

Perhaps if we were trained at a young age, we could access those skills in adulthood. My grand-mother, Anna Valentina, once said, "A child is like a flower. You start with the seed and give it a lot of love and attention. It will grow and bloom." Nurturing a child and providing meditation skills during youth may be quite beneficial throughout their school years and into adulthood.

One hundred years from now, it will not matter what my bank account was, how big my house was, or what kind of car I drove. But the world may be a little better because I was important in the life of a child.[54]

-Forest Witcraft

Dr. Forest E. Witcraft (1894 - 1967), was a scholar, teacher, and Boy Scout administrator.[55]

Disrobe yourself of any bad habits. It is said that it takes two weeks to change a habit.

---

[54] Witcraft, Forest, E. Quoteland.com
[55] Prince George's County Public Schools in www.pgcps.org

Please repeat, I WILL NOT ALLOW IMBALANCE TO DISRUPT MY HARMONY.

Chapter Five
Conformity

"CONFORMITY - Action in accordance with some specified standard or authority."[56]

If we accept and acquiesce in the face of discrimination, we accept the responsibility ourselves. We should, therefore, protest openly everything... that smacks discrimination or slander.[57]

>   -Mary McLeod Bethune
>   (July 10, 1875 –
>   May 18, 1955)

Mary McLeod Bethune's parents were slaves and she also worked the fields as a child. However, she had a desire and passion for

---

[56] Merriam-Webster.Com Dictionary

[57] Azquotes.com

education, and later became a civil rights activist and advisor to President Franklin D. Roosevelt. She then started a school for black students in Florida, which later became Bethune-Cookman University.[58]

Obedience is what we teach our children at a very young age. Rules and compliance keep children in line so they do not mature to be social misfits. Conduct is measured and evaluated throughout the educational years, as well as during employment, military service, and sports affiliations. Conduct and obedience along with conformity are important societal aspects.

However, conformity may not always be the best choice. It may be a road of discord. Consider historically when individuals conformed to the ill treatment of others and the many social injustices that occurred. Conformity may lead an individual to docility and weakness. An inability to venture toward change and suppress one's beliefs may lead to submission. The road to conformity and compliance may be a road less traveled by some. Where would we be without those involved in the fight for the rights of others? This brings to mind the song "I Hope You Dance" by Leeann Womack, words written by Mark D. Sanders and Tia Sillers. Amidst the lyrics are the words, "Never

---

[58] Biography.com

settle for the path of least resistance" and "When you come close to selling out, reconsider."[59] These poignant words can lead an individual through life. We are often taught conformity and obedience in our youthful years, but we hope in adulthood to strive for positive change. Speaking up and out will impact our world.

Conformity may lead to paralysis of both heart and action. We must push forward when we believe strongly about something and not allow others to stand in the way of change.

Rosa Parks was a woman of great strength and courage. Ms. Parks was an African-American seamstress residing in Alabama. During 1955 – a regrettable time of segregation among blacks and whites – Ms. Parks refused to give up her bus seat to a white man. While Ms. Parks spoke quietly, her words were heard loudly throughout the world. However, her nonconformity to relinquish her seat led her unjustly to jail. She was charged with disobeying the civil segregation laws of the state. Although she was later fired from her job, this pioneer paved the way during the civil rights movement. In 1956, the Supreme Court overturned and vacated the segregation laws, therefore allowing equality on buses. President William Clinton awarded Ms. Rosa

---

[59] Sanders and Sillers, I Hope You Dance.

Parks the Presidential Medal of Freedom in 1996. Rosa Parks died at the age of ninety-two during the year 2005.[60]

Harriet Ross was born into slavery in the early part of the 19th century. She was afflicted with beatings by white slave owners throughout her youth, before later marrying and becoming Harriet Tubman – the brave woman who escaped slavery.

She is responsible for the freedom of many slaves through her assistance in the Underground Railroad. As a fearless leader who moved slaves to a network of safe places along their freedom journeys, I still recall to this day the story of Ms. Harriet Tubman. In elementary school, I wrote a book report about her life, her struggles, and her strengths.

These are just a few of the many brave souls who rejected conformity for what they believed in. Their disobedience led to the wonderful changes in our country. Without their strength, advocacy, effort, and defiance, we would not have progressed as a society. While we remain a society of many imperfections, it is important that we deviate from and oppose that which we do not believe in and that which oppresses others. Nonconformance may mean struggle, but without such struggles our lives would not be

---

[60] Parks, Rosa

challenged. Living in a world of complete conformity would mean living in a dull world. Without it, we would not grow as individuals or flourish culturally. We must also speak for those whose voices have been silenced.

One may experience self-conformity when one acquiesces to negative self-talk and false beliefs. It may be a result of following the social norms of those surrounding you. An individual may have poor self-esteem as a result of self-conformity. Conforming to one's negative false beliefs can lead to a disruption in inner peace. It is also important that we as adults in-still positivity in our children rather than create a negative and harmful self-fulfilling prophecy. A self-fulfilling prophecy is when an individual believes the negative words he/she hears, and creates a negative picture of himself/herself as a result.

The ultimate measure of a man is not where he stands in moments of comfort, but where he stands at times of challenge and controversy.[61]

-Martin Luther King, Jr.

Dr. Martin Luther King Jr. was an African-American clergyman who shaped the American civil rights movement. He advocated for social change through

---

[61] King, Brainyquotes.com

non-violent means. Dr. Martin Luther King Jr. was murdered by a gunshot to his neck prior to leading a march protesting low wages and poor work conditions for sanitation workers in Tennessee in 1968. His assassin was an American – James Earl Ray. Ray pled guilty to the charge, and was sentenced to ninety-nine years in prison in 1969. Ray later recanted his guilty plea however, as there was no evidence to the contrary found, and died in prison in 1998.[62]

Please repeat, I WILL NOT ALLOW CONFORMITY TO DISRUPT MY HARMONY.

---

[62] Who2.com

Chapter Six
Hardship

"HARDSHIP - Something that causes or entails suffering or privation."[63]

Grief is a multifaceted response to loss. Although conventionally focused on the emotional response to loss, it also has physical, cognitive, behavioural, social and philosophical dimensions.[64]

Yesterday is gone. Tomorrow has not yet come. We have only today. Let us begin.[65]

-Mother Teresa

---

[63] Merriam-Webster.Com

[64] Wikipedia.org

[65] EWTN.org

During 1910, Agnes Gonxha Bojaxhiu was born in Macedonia. It is stated that during her adolescence, she received a calling from God. She later joined a group of nuns known as the Sisters of Loreto. Their focus was missionary work in India. Agnes later became known as Mother Teresa. She taught high school in Calcutta for many years and witnessed the extreme poverty and suffering of the Indian people. This led to a request she made to her superiors, asking to be with Calcutta's poor and suffering people. After this, Mother Teresa received permission to start her own order, "The Missionaries of Charity". Her lack of financial stability did not deter her mission, later receiving not only volunteers but also funding as well.

The Missionaries of Charity focused on caring for those who would otherwise be alone and discarded. Mother Teresa suffered and passed away from malaria and cardiac arrest at the age of eighty-seven on September 5, 1997.[66]

Hardship can present itself in many forms. One may experience emotional or physical suffering. The loss of a loved one can cause a great amount of grief. Such a loss may be due to a death

---

[66] Nobelprize.org

or estrangement, or perhaps the result of a separation or divorce. Individuals faced with the loss of a loved one may experience depression, isolation, and impairment in their normal functioning. A question comes up often about response to death and dying. What do you say to an individual who has lost a loved one? Some individuals I have treated in my practice who suffered from grief expressed irritability. Some state the irritability is a result of insensitive comments.

People may at times have difficulties expressing themselves. Often, it is not that they are trying to be insensitive or hurtful, they just do not know what to say. I have been told that it is bothersome to those who are grieving the loss of a child or parent when an individual says, "Well, they are better off because they are not suffering," or "I know what you are going through." We do not know what a person experiencing loss is going through, because each individual's story is unique and only they know how they feel. While we may have experienced loss in our own ways, we do not walk in the shoes of another.

I have found that what is most comforting to people experiencing loss is when one says, "I am sorry," and "Is there anything I can do for you?" Sometimes, words are not necessary. Just to be with another while he/she is grieving can be a great comfort and assistance. Many people who grieve have loved ones around them during the initial stages of their loss. They may be surrounded by friends and family. There may be services following the death of a loved one. Usually, the days following the final arrangements to put the person to their final resting place is when the realization affects the loved one. It is when the friends and family have gone home and there is silence.

Elizabeth Kübler-Ross was a world renowned psychiatrist who termed the stages of death. She focused on the stages that a terminally ill patient may experience. However, through the years, the stages of death have also been applied to those experiencing the death of a loved one. The stages are as follows:

1. Denial - The initial stage.: "It can't be happening."
2. Anger: "How dare you do this to me!" (either referring to God, the deceased, or oneself)
3. Bargaining: "Just let me live to see my son graduate."

4. Depression: "God, please don't take him away from our family."
5. Acceptance: "I know my son will be in a better place."[67]

Elizabeth Kübler-Ross applied these stages to any form of personal loss, such as the death of a loved one, or even divorce. These stages do not necessarily come in order, nor is each stage experienced by all patients. Kübler-Ross did believe that a person who experiences loss will experience at least two stages. Also, stages of grief may cross over with many occurring at the same time.

I would like to share with you my own experience of grief. Sadly, I lost grandparents and a few cousins in past years. I recall my first loss was my great-grandmother, and shortly following that my maternal grandfather. These were during my high school years, and I can still recall the empty feeling they left. I remember not wanting to do anything that I usually enjoyed, such as going out with friends. I lost my grandmother, Anna Valentina, at the age of eighty-five, a few years ago. She was a wonderful grandmother and our family matriarch. I believe I am accepting her death and

---

[67] Wikipedia.org

can say that I do not believe that I entered into the stages of anger or bargaining with respect to her death. Perhaps this is due to the fact that I watched her decline over the course of two years prior to her death.

Anna, or shall I say Nana – as many of her friends and family members called her – was a vibrant, loving, strong, opinionated, hardworking, kind, caring, compassionate, devoted, honest, anxious, and well-respected woman, to name a few of her qualities. She experienced much hardship in her lifetime, yet she never complained about it. As a child, she witnessed domestic violence in a home where her mother was beaten for talking back to her tyrannical husband. Nana once told me that she believed her father was a "good" and devoted father, yet she could not understand his abuse toward her mother. She shared her thoughts and questioned her father's love as he was abusive toward his wife. She and her siblings witnessed his abuse.

It was not often that she spoke about her childhood, because it caused her great pain. She became tearful at times and stated that she preferred not to discuss her past. One particular day, though, she decided to share her memories. She spoke about a day she returned home from school to find her mother crying in a corner near the out-side cement steps. Nana proceeded to tell me the reason behind her mother's tears. She explained that her father struck her mother for drying the children's clothing too close to the stove. This wife and mother of six received beatings by her hus-band and often their children witnessed the vio-lence. Nana also stated that her mother would be struck again when she "answered her husband back". Nana said that she too would be punished for interfering and supporting her mother against her father. However, she denied that her father struck her or abused his children. She often spoke highly of him and remained quite loyal. Perhaps it was her father's loyalty to his children.

They lived during the difficult times of the Great Depression. There was little money, and her father was forced to place his children temporar-ily at the state orphanage when their mother was hospitalized. Nana explained that he visited every weekend and promised to take his children home as soon as possible. Nana recalled the female and male children being separated within the or-phanage.

She painted a sad picture of their separation and longing to talk as siblings do. However, they were not able to. Instead, she would wave to her brother across the courtyard. Their father sold apples and took any possible work he could to save money. He saved every penny to secure enough money to take his children home. Nana's mother was institutionalized, in what was then called an "insane asylum". It was the age of the "hysterical woman" and little was known or discussed about domestic violence. Women were institutionalized in a male dominated society where they may have been outspoken and unruly during the culture of male domination.

This abused mother of six resided in a state operated mental institution until her death during the early 20th century. The stigma of mental illness was prominent during that time. Women who were considered "hysterical" may have been hospitalized or institutionalized for their behaviors or outspokenness. There was no mention or consideration of Acute Stress or Posttraumatic Stress during those years. That era assumed that one unable to cope with life was crazy or insane. There was little understanding of precipitants to one's functional decline or that physical abuse may have been the cause. It was a Freudian time of neurotic women, victim blaming and misrepresentation.

It was not until the 1980s that the diagnosis of Posttraumatic Stress Disorder (PTSD) was established. One may have associated a PTSD diagnosis with a war Veteran. While this has been one population who may suffer from post trauma, it is certainly not the only. The Posttraumatic Stress Disorder definition found in the DSM-V is as follows:

DSM-5 Criteria for PTSD

In 2013, the American Psychiatric Association revised the PTSD diagnostic criteria in the fifth edition of its Diagnostic and Statistical Manual of Mental Disorders (DSM-5)[1]. The diagnostic criteria are specified below.

Note that DSM-5 introduced a preschool subtype of <u>PTSD for children ages six years and younger</u>. The criteria below are specific to adults, adolescents, and children older than six years. Diagnostic criteria for PTSD include a history of exposure to a traumatic event that meets specific stipulations and symptoms from each of four symptom clusters: intrusion, avoidance, negative alterations in cognitions and mood, and alterations in arousal and reactivity. The sixth criterion concerns duration of symptoms; the seventh *assesses functioning; and, the eighth crite-rion clarifies symptoms as not attributable to a substance or co-occurring medical condi-tion. Two specifications are noted, including delayed expression and a <u>dissociative sub-type of PTSD</u> – the latter of which is new to DSM-5. In both specifications, the full diag-nostic criteria for PTSD must be met for a warranted diagnosis.*

Criterion A: stressor

The person was exposed to: death, threat-ened death, actual or threatened serious in-jury, or actual or threatened sexual violence, as follows (one required):

1. Direct exposure.

2. Witnessing, in person.

3. Indirectly, by learning that a close rela-tive or close friend was exposed to trauma. If the event involved actual or threatened death, it must have been violent or accidental.

4. Repeated or extreme indirect exposure to aversive details of the event(s), usu-ally in the course of professional du-ties (e.g., first responders, collecting body parts; professionals repeatedly exposed to details of child abuse). This does not include indirect non-profes-sional exposure through electronic media, television, movies, or pictures.

Criterion B: intrusion symptoms

The traumatic event is persistently re-experi-enced in the following way(s) (one required):

1. *Recurrent, involuntary, and intrusive memories. Note: Children older than six may express this symptom in re-petitive play.*
2. *Traumatic nightmares. Note: Children may have frightening dreams without content related to the trauma(s).*
3. *Dissociative reactions (e.g., flashbacks) which may occur on a continuum from brief episodes to complete loss of consciousness. Note: Children may reenact the event in play.*
4. *Intense or prolonged distress after ex-posure to traumatic reminders.*
5. *Marked physiologic reactivity after ex-posure to trauma-related stimuli.*

Criterion C: avoidance

Persistent effortful avoidance of distressing trauma-related stimuli after the event (one required):

1. *Trauma-related thoughts or feelings.*
2. *Trauma-related external reminders (e.g., people, places, conversations, activities, objects, or situations).*

Criterion D: negative alterations in cognitions and mood

Negative alterations in cognitions and mood that began or worsened after the traumatic event (two required):

1. *Inability to recall key features of the traumatic event (usually dissociative amnesia; not due to head injury, alcohol, or drugs).*
2. *Persistent (and often distorted) negative beliefs and expectations about oneself or the world (e.g., "I am bad," "The world is completely dangerous").*
3. *Persistent distorted blame of self or others for causing the traumatic event or for resulting consequences.*
4. *Persistent negative trauma-related emotions (e.g., fear, horror, anger, guilt, or shame).*

5. *Markedly diminished interest in (pre-traumatic) significant activities.*
6. *Feeling alienated from others (e.g., detachment or estrangement).*
7. *Constricted affect: persistent inability to experience positive emotions.*

Criterion E: alterations in arousal and reactivity

Trauma-related alterations in arousal and reactivity that began or worsened after the traumatic event (two required):

1. *Irritable or aggressive behavior*
2. *Self-destructive or reckless behavior*
3. *Hypervigilance*
4. *Exaggerated startle response*
5. *Problems in concentration*
6. *Sleep disturbance*

Criterion F: duration

Persistence of symptoms (in Criteria B, C, D, and E) for more than one month.

Criterion G: functional significance

Significant symptom-related distress or functional impairment (e.g., social, occupational).

Criterion H: exclusion

Disturbance is not due to medication, substance use, or other illness.

Specify if: With dissociative symptoms.

In addition to meeting criteria for diagnosis, an individual experiences high levels of either of the following in reaction to trauma-related stimuli:

1. *Depersonalization: experience of being an outside observer of or detached from oneself (e.g., feeling as if "this is not happening to me" or one were in a dream).*
2. *Derealization: experience of unreality, distance, or distortion (e.g., "things are not real").*

Specify if: With delayed expression.

Full diagnosis is not met until at least six months after the trauma(s), although onset of symptoms may occur immediately.[68] An Acute Stress Disorder diagnosis may be more suitable within the month following a trauma exposure. Acute Stress and Post Traumatic Stress symptoms may overlap. Some

---

[68] DSM-5

individuals may also experience diagnoses of more than one illness. An example of this would be PTSD and Major Depressive Disorder. It is important to understand that trauma and depression can exist separately, and one may have nothing to do with the other.

A woman is like a tea bag. You never know how strong she is until she's in hot water.
                              -Eleanor Roosevelt[69]

Hardship may come in various forms. Marital, financial, grief and misfortune to name a few. Some societal opinions consider divorce as failure which brings hardship to individuals and their children – when in reality, this may or may not be the case. Actually, those who remain in dysfunctional and demeaning relationships may experience feelings of failure, distress, and hardship. It appears some individuals remain in the relationship due to economic strains, while some remain together because of the cost of

[69] Home.Att.Net

separation and two households. The financial burden may be less with one household versus two.

Far away there in the sunshine are my highest aspirations. I may not reach them, but I can look up and see their beauty, believe in them, and try to follow where they lead.[70]

-Louisa May Alcott

Louisa May Alcott helped her family's financial troubles by working at a young age. She later began writing and authored *Little Women,* based on her life growing up in a New England town in the 1800s. I had the opportunity to visit the Lousia May Alcott home in Concord, Massachusetts with my mother and grandmother many years ago. She was actually Nana's favorite writer.

There are no mistakes, no coincidences. All events are blessings given to us to learn from.[71]

-Elizabeth Kubler-Ross

---

[70] Bookreporter.com

[71] Goodreads

Please repeat, I WILL NOT ALLOW HARDSHIP TO DISRUPT MY HARMONY.

Chapter Seven
Chaos

"CHAOS - A state of utter confusion or disorder; a total lack of organization or order."[72]

It's a lack of clarity that creates chaos and frustration. Those emotions are poison to any living goal.[73]

-Steven Maraboli,
Life, the Truth, and
Being Free.

Steven Maraboli is a United States Air Force Veteran, motivational speaker, philanthropist, and bestselling author.

---

[72] Dictionary.com
[73] Maraboli, 2009

When we discuss the opposite of chaos, we may consider the words; orderly, tidy, and organized. Chaos may be brief in an individual's life, or it may be ongoing. I like to call the latter, chronic chaos. Chaos that is ongoing may be considered chronic chaos. Some individuals thrive on chronic chaos, and find it difficult to live otherwise. It may be considered a codependent relationship in some ways. The individual struggles to live outside the confusion, just like the codependent partner may find it difficult without the dysfunctional relationship. Chaos may be found in one's mind, home, relationship, and/or work life. Chaos may cause disruption to healthy functioning over time. While at times it is unavoidable, how we press forward and recover from it is quite significant. It is important to determine best practices with respect to chaos.

Let us take for example Theresa and Pat. Both women despise chaos and believe in order and organization. Both have lived their lives this way, having been role models and taught family best orderly practices. While of different generations and not even related, they have similarities in their organization. Pat's belief is that what may take time at the onset will, in fact, lessen over time. Those who know and love her admire her for her ability to multitask and make it look simple. Her home is always immaculate, and she cooks homemade meals daily. These are not simple meals; rather, they are elaborate ones. Pat may be found simmering fresh soups with various ingredients, or cooking meat and pasta dishes.

Whatever the meal may be, it will surely be made of the freshest ingredients. She caters to her family and does this while working full time. It is the same with Theresa; she manages her time while keeping at the forefront the importance of family, good food, and her career. Both teach us the importance of mustering the energy to complete the tasks at the onset rather than procrastinating – because procrastination may lead to future chaos. Outer chaos may also contribute to inner chaos.

Clutter within your environment and daily surroundings will certainly impact your inner tranquility.

During the course of my clinical practice, some clients discussed chaotic households. I present this in no way to judge any individual, but rather to understand and learn from their experiences.

One individual in particular – we will call her Susan – indicated that her home was quite cluttered. What was reported appeared to be hoarding. I say "appeared" because I do not physically enter into a client's home. Clients' appointments are scheduled at my private practice location. This particular client discussed limiting visitors due to the condition of her home. She stated that friends visited from time to time, only with advance notice and with visits confined to one area in her home. She reported ongoing clutter that caused her great embarrassment. Under no circumstances were others allowed in other rooms within her home – not even her boyfriend.

Susan had a significant other who would not visit her home; rather, she would visit his home. Treatment plan goals were discussed and included consistent home cleaning and decluttering. We also developed a plan with steps to include organization.

This presented some challenges at the beginning. Susan expressed feeling overwhelmed by the thought of organizing. Feeling distressed and overwhelmed may be common for those living a chaotic existence. Sometimes half the battle is just recognizing certain feelings and identifying them. Our plan was to begin her organization process with small spaces. If her kitchen was unorganized, we started with her kitchen table. This helps individuals feel a bit less overpowered.

When one enters a cluttered environment, it is overwhelming and difficult to know where to begin decluttering. Starting with a small space can lead to better organization and less anxiety. This client in particular felt overwhelmed by her surroundings. Her anxieties surrounding this increased when she thought about where and how to begin cleaning. Taking on a small space initially made it less bothersome.

If you are struggling with chaos and disorganization, take steps to reorganize. This may feel completely distressing, and for some even paralyzing. Find someone you trust to help you over the hurdle. Perhaps a friend can assist you so that you are not alone while reorganizing. If you cannot consider anyone to help you, consider hiring a professional. This may be your answer, and may alleviate any stress. If you are able to begin the process yourself, start with a very small area. Once that area is straightened out, move to the next.

You may want to pick up some reading materials as an aid. Marie Kondo, is a Japanese organizer who has written books and can be found on her Netflix Series, *Tidying Up with Marie Kondo.* Marie's method of organizing is called the "KonMari Method" and considers keeping items that bring joy rather than just focusing on items you need to get rid of. The is a new approach for some and lessens a bit of the burden. Bringing the focus to joy rather than dislike may be a more creative approach. We are all capable of creating change.

In The Hands of Man

He who creates a poison, also has the cure. He who creates a virus, also has the antidote.

He who creates chaos, also has the ability to create peace.

He who sparks hate, also has the ability to transform it to love.

He who creates misery, also has the ability to destroy it with kindness.
He who creates sadness, also has the ability to convert it to happiness.

He who creates darkness, can also be awakened to produce illumination.

He who spreads fear, can also be shaken to spread comfort.

Any problems created by the left hand of man, can also be solved with the right. For he who manifests anything, also has the ability to Destroy it."[74]

> -Suzy Kassem, *Rise Up and Salute the Sun: The Writings of Suzy Kassem*

---

[74] Suzy Kassem, *Rise Up and Salute the Sun: The Writings of Suzy Kassem.*

Experiences may feel chaotic as we move through the chaos, even if done in an organized manner. War is an example of this.

War may feel disorderly in its confusion but very organized in its approach. The "fog" of war may be an example of this. "War is the realm of uncertainty; three quarters of the factors on which action in war is based are wrapped in a fog of greater or lesser uncertainty. A sensitive and discriminating judgment is called for; a skilled intelligence to scent out the truth."[75]

Although I never served in the military, I spent part of my career serving Veterans in a clinical capacity. I also share my life with a Marine who served in Desert Storm. I recall his "fog of war" description that soldiers may experience during combat. He explained his struggles during battle engagements, which included positive self talk. "I would say to myself: 'I just want to make it past this cloud and move toward the horizon ahead.'"[76] He explained how his focus was on the here and now – one cloud at a time – and he would not allow himself to project much further than that. I have also witnessed how he uses this analogy toward other aspects of this life.

---

[75] Carl von Clausewitz, On War, 1832

[76] Glenmore Wagner, 2019

While multiple projects and stressors may lie ahead, he keeps focused on the immediate. Looking far into the distance may cause one to feel overwhelmed. Going beyond what is directly in front of you during intense situations and especially combat situations may increase one's stress level. While it is important to have a plan, and in particular – a battlefield mission in warfare – it may be just as necessary to keep the focus on what is near. Target what is directly in sight, while also finding balance with what's ahead. We cannot move so quickly through chaos in an attempt to bring order without also taking some time easing our way forward.

We need to slow down at times to clear the clutter and chaos. This replenishes us in many ways, including our souls. The *150 Most Important Bible Verses* chapter, "Quiet Amid Chaos" explains, "Slow Down. Avoid being so busy with necessities of life that you forget to nourish your soul."[77]

Please repeat, I WILL NOT ALLOW CHAOS TO DISRUPT MY HARMONY.

---

[77] The 150 Most Important Bible Verses

Chapter Eight
Self-Esteem

"SELF-ESTEEM - Belief and confidence in your own ability and value."[78]

You gain strength, courage, and confidence by every experience in which you really stop to look fear in the face. You are able to say to yourself, "I have lived through this horror. I can take the next thing that comes along."...You must do the thing you think you cannot do.[79]

-Eleanor Roosevelt

Eleanor Roosevelt was the wife of President Franklin Delano Roosevelt. First Lady Roosevelt was a human rights activist who was well

---

[78] Cambridge Dictionary
[79] Quoteland.com

loved and respected, not only in the United States but also throughout the world.

With each step we take toward our life goals, we often gain confidence. We become more and more confident as our skills develop. If a child is constantly berated and hears negative comments, she or he may begin believing such criticisms. One may develop what is called a negative self-fulfilling prophecy. A self-fulfilling prophecy is when thoughts affect expectations, which in turn influence outcomes. The individual believes the comment about him/herself and begins to act in a way conducive to that belief.

Alternatively, when comments are complimentary they can elevate self-esteem. Let us consider the Laws of Attraction. The Laws of Attraction indicate that the more we believe something, the greater likelihood it will come our way. "It really does take many negative thoughts and persistent negative thinking to bring something negative into your life. However, if you persist in thinking negative thoughts over a period of time, they *will* appear in your life."[80] Therefore, the child provided a foundation of continued positive reinforcements will have a greater likelihood of good self-esteem. This does not mean, however, that we tell lies to always magnify one's self-esteem.

---

[80] The Secret, Byrne, page 22.

We must be truthful and kind in our approach. Being provided habitual praise may grow an ego and be just as damaging as negative ridicule. An inflated self-image and "inflated sense of self" may provide false hope and arrogance when approaching goals. What is most important is a balanced sense of self.

Self and the ego go far back in the world of psychology. From what I recall, the ego was formed in early childhood and connected with one's experiences. A fractured sense of self may be found with individuals diagnosed with borderline personality disorders. Such an individual usually struggles with their own identities and feelings. There may be difficulty regulating emotions. Such individuals may express polar opposites from day to day, they love the person today and hate the same person tomorrow. This can be quite frustrating and confusing to the loved one. Tolerating and regulating feelings for the individual diagnosed with Borderline Personality Disorder can be a struggle. Intensive therapy is often necessary.

One must learn to find the balance between thoughts and emotions while learning to tolerate feelings and vulnerabilities that may surface with emotions. Exercises can help the individual recognize and identify emotions while understanding that just as they surfaced, they will also leave. Understanding and withstanding thoughts and emotions is beneficial. Tapping into emotions and realizing while they are a part of you, they are not the whole you. Just as they come to you, they will leave.

This may help individuals who are so affected by emotions and feelings that they fear they will remain a part of their daily lives. Rejecting and blocking without facing certain emotions and feelings will not be productive over time. We must feel our feelings and face any discomfort while realizing this too will pass.

Marsha Linehan is a clinician who specifically addresses the needs of individuals with borderline personality disorders. She provides exercises which are actually beneficial to all individuals, not just those with psychiatric disorders. Ms. Linehan is a psychologist who developed Dialectical Behavior Therapy – also known as DBT.

DBT is more intensive than CBT – which is Cognitive Behavior Therapy. DBT may include weekly individual and group sessions where one may focus on emotion regulation to include mindfulness and radical acceptance within the clinical treatment. Ms. Linehan also authored *Cognitive-Behavioral Treatment for Borderline Personality Disorder and Skills Training Manual for Treating Borderline Personality Disorder.*

Ms. Linehan's tools may be used by anyone, regardless of whether or not the individual has a Borderline Personality Disorder diagnosis. No one is exempt from life's pain and struggles. In this way, Marsha Linehan coined the term, "Radical Acceptance". It basically encourages one during meditation to accept your life in the moment completely; accepting the bad with the good. I use her materials quite often within my clinical practice as I attended several training sessions through the years. The content still remains of great significance and allows one to let go and be in the moment during mindfulness. Mindfulness is about being present completely, while letting go of any thoughts or influences. It encourages you to be in the here and now without attempting to change anything.

For clients interested in mindful meditation, I ask them to find a quiet place and a comfortable spot where there will be no interruptions. Try this yourself and inform any family who reside in your home to allow you some quiet, uninterrupted time alone. Turn off your phone and any background noise, including music and television. Once a tranquil space is located, sit comfortably on the floor with some pillows. If one is unable to do this, perhaps you can sit in a chair or recline somehow. You may want to place a pillow on your lap for comfort.

Begin with some cleansing breaths in and out. My years of dance training have contributed quite a bit to my clinical practice exercises. I often use some dance methods within the clinical session. Clients are asked to focus on each body part as I take them through a relaxation exercise. We start with the forehead and isolate that part of the body. I will ask that they contract and release the forehead. Close your eyes and squeeze your forehead slightly, and then release. Travel next to your face; contract and release. Slowly move your way from the top of your head to the bottom of your feet. Take time to isolate each body part with a contraction and a release.

This is my recommendation for the start of a meditation session. Each person must feel comfortable and design a plan that best suits them.

Once the initial exercise is completed, I recommend either a visual or breathing meditation exercise to follow. Marsha Linehan describes a tree with a stream below. One is to focus on the leaf and have it float, placing any thoughts on the leaf. I like to go a bit further, though.

Initially, I ask that you create a picture in your mind. Imagine a beautiful fall foliage as long as you are comfortable with this picture. I always ask clients to be sure they are comfortable with the picture/image and be sure that it does not trigger a bad memory in any way. Once this is determined, visualize a beautiful warm autumn day with colorful leaves engulfing a tree. Now try to bring your focus to one particular leaf. Focus on its shape and any markings it may have while looking at its colorful shades. How does its stem connect to the tree and what makes it unique? A warm breeze moves the leaf slowly from its place on the tree, and it begins to fall ever so slightly to the stream below. Picture the leaf floating, slowly moving its way through the water. Place any thoughts or worries on the leaf and watch it float away. Continue to repeat this exercise daily.

The narcissistic individual – one with an inflated self-esteem – has just as much difficulty as the person with a negative sense of self. I recall Heinz Kohut's self psychology concepts and the impact of an inflated sense of self and narcissism. Kohut discussed the evolving relationships between children and their parents with his concepts. "Heinz Kohut asserts that adult narcissistic psychopathology is a result of parental lack of empathy during development."[81] Basically, the parent is so self absorbed that he/she is not meeting the emotional needs of the child. However, lack of empathy may not necessarily be within an individual's control.

---

[81] McLean, 2007

One may be depressed and therefore not able to respond properly to the child's emotional needs. This, however, does not mean that all depressed parents do not meet their children's needs and have negative self-images. Many are quite capable and able. The narcissist, however, keeps the focus on him/herself. Again, this can be just as damaging as the individual with a poor self-esteem. Balance is the key. Regarding poor self-esteem, build your self-esteem initially to a place where you feel good about yourself. It is not necessary to have an elevated self-image, but it certainly is good to have a positive one. Building a positive self-image takes consistent practice. Experiences contribute to the development of one's self-image. Keeping a positive flow of incoming positivity is quite important.

Positive affirmations may assist with building positive self-images. Write a few positive sentences and repeat them throughout the course of your day.

I often discuss this with clients, actually asking them to place what they write on sticky notes or pieces of paper. I ask men and women to place the positive words in their billfolds or pocketbooks. They are asked to recite the words or sentences throughout their day. I find that individuals often struggled with this. Initially, clients have difficulties finding positive words about themselves and then even more difficulties sharing it with someone else. The other difficulty was that people often forget to place it in their wallets or pocketbooks, therefore, they are not able to recite it daily. This led to my creation of a positive word product company called alEgeEmpower.com.

Confidence is the hinge on the door to success.
-Mary O'Hare Dumas[82]

Please repeat, I WILL NOT ALLOW SELF-ESTEEM TO DISRUPT MY HARMONY.

---

[82] Dumas, O'Hare Mary

Chapter Nine
Greed

"GREED - A selfish and excessive desire for more of something (such as money) than is needed."[83]

The fragrance always stays in the hand that gives the rose.[84]

-Hada Bejar

Hada Bejar was a Cuban actress born in the 1930s. She passed away in 2014.

Greed can certainly interfere with your harmony. Ongoing overindulgence when one misses the fullness of giving may move you in a negative direction. One may certainly strive without being greedy.

---

[83] Merriam-Webster.Com Dictionary

[84] Good News Network 2018.

However, one may also be ambitious without being greedy. One may even be successful and wealthy without being greedy. It is wonderful for the individual who is a financial success and able to share his/her wealth. Being overly self-indulgent and self-centered is all consuming.

You must consider where you wish to focus your attention and love. For some, it may be money, and for others it may be people. If one is all consumed with obtaining more financially well above what is needed, it may lead to excess and waste. We all need to maintain financial stability. However, is there ever really enough money? Can we do without the next purchase? If working to the point of exhaustion and perhaps missing out on family obligations, you may want to re-evaluate. The years really do pass quickly; as we blink, our children are grown. Can you really afford to miss out on your child's next school performance or sports event? Do you make the effort to be fully present during momentous occasions? Being present means turning off your cell phone and experiencing the moment completely. Your children will be aware of this, even if they do not say it. They will notice and feel you being all in and all present.

While mindful moments may not be considered traditional meditation, it still is mindfulness. It is being in the mindful moment completely. Mindfulness focuses your awareness on something, wherever you may be. One does not need the typical and traditional meditation sitting posture or setting for mindfulness. You may be driving to work and instead of thinking about what you have to do once you arrive, be mindful and present of your experience. If it is driving, see what is ahead and feel the steering wheel while you have both hands grasping it.

Mindfulness is also about letting go of any judgements. One may do this during mindfulness and/or meditation. It is very important to let go, without judgement of yourself or others while giving the moment and situation your complete undivided attention.

Let's take a walk as an example. Next time you go for a walk, pay attention to what occurs. Are you going through lists in your mind of what needs to be done later? Are you thinking about something that occurred at home or work? Now, consider a different approach. Totally immerse yourself as you walk using some of your five senses. Try sight, hearing, and smell during your next stroll. Really look at the scenery along your walk. Identify what you see? What's in your environment? Take time to notice the different colors your eyes spot. Really take more time than a glimpse or a glance. You may even consider touch as you reach for a leaf or feel a tree along the way. Do you hear or smell anything? Also, the next time you cook a meal or bake something, try a mindful experience. Hone your skills and ability to focus on your sense of touch, smell, and taste. Witness the difference it makes for your experience.

...For myself, I think the greatest happiness of this life is to be released from the cares and formalities of what is called the world. My world is my family, and all the change to me will be that I can devote myself unmolested to my treasure.[85]

Letting go of the monetary influences may not be easy. We need to pay our bills and buy our groceries. We need to work hard to succeed. We are taught that idleness is unsatisfactory.

We must strive and be driven. Yes, ambition is wonderful! It motivates us to do better in life. However, it must be balanced as most everything. When it becomes excessive, it becomes a life disruptor. It becomes a disruptor of harmony.

Is greed disrupting your harmony? If so, re-evaluate and fine-tune where needed. If you are unsure, perhaps ask a loved one or friend. If you struggle to sort through it yourself, you may wish to reach out to a professional. Do you

---

[85] St. Elizabeth Seton, 1992. Compiled by Ronda De Sola Chervin. CMJ Marian Publishers. *Quotable Saints*

have insurance? The backside of your insurance card should have a telephone number for counseling information. If you do not know a counselor or psychotherapist, you may call the number on the back of your card for referral information. If you work for a company, they may partner with an Employee Assistance Program that you may contact. You may also ask someone you know if they are familiar with any therapists in the area or perhaps try Google. Clinicians, psychotherapists, and counselors are usually similar. However, there may be differences in their licenses and approaches. You should consider what his/her background and licensure is. If someone is not certified and licensed by the state you reside in, you may wish to consider another clinician.

There are some very successful companies who demonstrate to us that there can be great financial gain and success while remaining balanced with what is important in life. A good example of this is Chick-fil-A. The company does not open on Sundays so that employees may worship if they wish and spend time with family. Hobby Lobby is another company who chooses to remain closed on Sundays. It is quite evident that these companies would profit enormously on Sundays, but their beliefs outweigh their pockets. They are examples demonstrating to us that you can be successful without being greedy. Both Chick-fil-A and Hobby Lobby are financially stable companies. Hobby Lobby founder, David Green wrote the book, *Giving It All Away...and Getting It All Back Again: The Way of Living Generously.* The author describes Hobby Lobby as the largest arts and crafts store worldwide that is privately owned and grosses more than $5 billion dollars annually.[86]

Please repeat, I WILL NOT ALLOW GREED TO DISRUPT MY HARMONY.

---

[86] Green, David and High, Bill. 2017. Zondervan. *Giving It All Away...and Getting It All Back Again: The Way of Living Generously.*

Chapter Ten
Apathy

"APATHY - 1. Lack of feeling or emotion: impassive-ness; 2. Lack of interest or concern: indifference"[87]

Compassion is a jewel.[88]

-The Dalai Lama

The present day Dalai Lama, Tenzin Gyatso, is the 14th Dalai Lama of Tibet. He was born Lhamo Thondup in 1935 to farming parents. He became the Dalai Lama at age two when he was selected by the thirteenth Dalai Lama. He fled Tibet

---

[87] Merriam-Webster.Com Dictionary

[88] Dalai Lama. 2002. *How to Practice the Way to a Meaningful Life*, His Holiness the Daila Lama, Translated and Edited by Jeffrey Hopkins, Ph.D.

in his early 20s to seek asylum in India where he presently resides. He is also a recipient of the 1989 Nobel Peace Prize and 2006 Congressional Gold Medal.

I had the distinct privilege of meeting and listening to the Dalai Lama some years back. His Holiness spoke during a clinical conference held in Boston, Massachusetts. The lecture, hosted by Harvard Medical School, focused on meditation and psychotherapy. The year was 2009, and the panel discussion included compassion and wisdom. The Dalai Lama sat alongside some renowned clinicians, including Jon Kabat-Zin and Marsha Linehan – mentioned earlier in this book. My colleagues Kate and Jo-Ann attended as well. It was quite poignant as Kate and I attended graduate school together years earlier, wondering what our future clinical experiences would be.

Jo-Ann and I started our careers in the early 1990s when we both were employed by Brown University's Psychiatric Research Department. We worked on various psychiatric studies as research assistants. Jo-Ann went on to further her education in the area of psychology to become a psychologist. Today, we all remain practicing psychotherapists.

Vividly, I recall becoming so excited when I learned that the Dalai Lama was staying at our hotel. I almost acted like a young girl following a celebrity around. He was surrounded by bodyguards and not very approachable. His face was quite pleasant though, with a nice smile and he did not appear as serious as I would have imagined. His robe colors were my favorites; shades of orange and yellow. I was ecstatic when I learned that not only was he staying in our hotel, but that his room was actually on my floor. He was surrounded by many bodyguards; some posted at each elevator while others were outside his room.

Jo-Ann and I waited patiently trying not to look too conspicuous, often returning to our rooms to seem less obvious. We were determined to meet him as he left his room. We finally did! Our timing was perfect and we were able to greet him at the elevators. I was steadfast in capturing a picture but he was protected by staff. My respectful request for a quick cell phone photograph was granted. Just as he entered the elevator, I snapped my picture. Later, I was disappointed to discover the one and only picture taken was very poor quality. My memories of the experience will have to suffice. I remain grateful for my experience. It was a wonderful opportunity to listen as he spoke to a crowd of clinicians explaining how best to educate our clients about meditation. I found him very humble, often asking clinicians what their thoughts were to questions he received.

In How to Practice, The Way to a Meaningful Life, His Holiness the Dalai Lama, "As Shantideva's *A Guide to the Bodhisattva Way of Life* says, if a blind person finds a jewel in a pile of garbage, she would cherish it dearly. If, in the midst of the garbage of lust, hatred, and ignorance-emotions that afflict our own minds and our world, we generate compassionate attitude, we should cherish this like a jewel."[89] The story goes on to speak about enlightenment and how monetary gifts and gains may be brief and not bring true satisfaction and tranquility long term. It is the deeper understanding and enlightenment of what a "true jewel" is. Compassion and empathy creates a greater sense of being and connectedness in our lives.

In the Dalai Lama's chapter "Aspiring to Enlightenment," he points out that "Compassion is the key to achieving a deeper level of morality"[90]. Our morals shape us, influencing our everyday interactions and decisions. The molding begins during childhood. May our morals change over time? Certainly; we learn, we grow, and we mature. This is not to say that our morals cannot change in a less desired direction. Yes, they may change in a negative direction as well. Perhaps they started out pure and good, but became tainted

---

[89] Ibid

[90] Ibid

over time. Our morals shape us along with our experiences.

When I think of apathy, I think of the opposite: empathy. While empathy is sharing the feelings another one is experiencing, apathy is having little interest in them. Such indifference over time will certainly disrupt your harmony.

An experience I had while living in New York City for a short while comes to mind. I subleased an apartment on Manhattan's Upper West Side from a friend who was attending the Juilliard School. It was the summer of 1989, and I was determined to love every minute of my experience. Quickly, I became aware of the harsh realities – as this was a culture shock for me coming from a small town in the U.S.'s smallest state. I witnessed a man slice another man's pants pocket and run off with the money he stole. I watched as people just continued walking over and beside the injured man who remained on the ground. Nobody stopped to help him up or ask if he was hurt. I stood paralyzed myself, but was mostly bewildered by the fact that not one individual assisted this victim. I did not help him; I guess fear set in for me as a young woman. I quickly moved along myself to get away from the situation. Some guilt surrounding my inaction to assist another in need remained. I do not know if someone did finally help that man, but I surely hope so. Years later while studying at graduate school, I learned about the murder of Kitty Genovese.

Ms. Genovese was a young female in her 20s residing in New York during the 1960s. She was raped and stabbed to death outside her Queens apartment. Her screams for help went unresponded to by numerous neighbors. Why would others be so indifferent as to allow another human being to be attacked without even an attempt to contact the police? Many who supposedly heard the screams were in the comfort of their own apartments. Their own safety was not in jeopardy yet, so they failed to empathize and aid Ms. Genovese by a simple telephone call to the police. Instead, she suffered and died.

In situations like this, terms such as "bystander effect" and "bystander apathy" come to mind. The bystander effect means there is less likelihood for someone to assist an individual in need when there is a greater number of people present. This may have been the situation I experienced while residing in New York City. The street was crowded, and there was hustle and bustle. Bystander apathy may have taken place. However, in the case of Kitty Genovese, people were inside their apartments and unaware of how many others may have heard the attack. The incident was later mentioned in many psychological articles and her story was shared in many clinical settings. Numerous factors may be relevant concerning incident reactions. We cannot judge and say for sure that those who do not respond to the aid of another are apathetic. We would need to further explore the reasons behind their inaction.

Apathy over time – or chronic apathy – will impact your mood and happiness. It may produce negative ramifications and lessen one's happiness.

Author Marci Shimoff writes about happiness. In *Secrets of the Masters, The Missing Factor... Happiness* article, she reports, "Marci's Inner Home of Happiness:

1. Foundation: Take responsibility for your life; take ownership of your own happiness.
2. Pillar of the Mind: Don't believe everything you think; your beliefs can hold you back from achieving happiness.
3. Pillar of the Heart: Let love lead in your life.
4. Pillar of the Body: Make your body happy, beginning with your cells; invest energy and healthy food in your body.
5. Pillar of the Soul: Plug yourself into Spirit; connect to something bigger than yourself.
6. Roof: Live an inspired life; find ways to serve yourself and to serve others in the world."[91]

---

[91] Shimoff, Marci. Secrets of the Masters: The Missing Factor....Happiness

Happiness may be the new car, big house, or large bank account for some. These items may bring some gratification but it may not last indefinitely. Happiness comes from within; and may not be from external factors. Most often, unhappiness is not due to a lack of being without something. In her book, *Happy For No Reason*, Marci points out that 40% of happiness is habit, while 10% is circumstances, and the other 50% is genetic. Therefore, we can control over 40% of our happiness by changing our habits, learned thoughts, and behaviors.

Wendy Wood, a habit researcher and professor at USC, reported that over 40% of daily behaviors are habits.[92] New habits are able to be formed by repeating them. Just under half of habits occur because they are performed in the same place. When working with clients diagnosed with trichotillomania, I ask them to keep a hair-pulling journal. Time and again, clients find themselves pulling often in the same location, perhaps their home or car, for example.

We often make behavioral modification changes. This is not to say that chronic hair pulling is a habit; however, there are components, which are habit-formed. Many people believe hair pulling occurs during states of intense anxiety or frustration. However, it

---

[92] Team Clarizen. 2019.

is often quite the opposite – individuals may find themselves in a relaxed state, watching television, only to find themselves pulling their hair. We will not get into trichotillomania at this point, for this is a topic and book for itself. My point is, if you are attempting to change your habits, you may wish to consider your behaviors. Changing behavioral components may influence the habits we form.

Healthandwellnesscoaching.org provides a pdf with a free "Happy For No Reason Workbook" and happiness questionnaire. Rate your happiness! A gratitude practice is quite important. It combats apathy in many ways as it provides introspection and thankfulness to others. Try this for yourself: keep a journal with gratitude entries. You may return to it during difficult days when you have forgotten all you are grateful for.

"Nearly every day, we may have an opportunity to give something to someone—our time, our love, or our resources. I have always found more joy in giving when I did not expect anything in return."[93]

Please repeat, I WILL NOT ALLOW APATHY TO DISRUPT MY HARMONY.

---

[93] Cathy, S. Truett

Please consider the disruptors of harmony in your life and envision how changes will be made. Realize that we all have moments of disruption and distress, but the question is whether or not it is ongoing. If so, consider what adjustments you can make and how to move forward with positive changes. Also, think about quotes that come to mind, and consider those who wrote and experienced disruptors in their pasts.

Please also include alternate pronouns to suit your preference. Let us all strive to achieve the "Success" Bessie speaks to.

Success

He has achieved success
who has lived well,
laughed often, and loved much;
who has enjoyed the trust of pure women,
the respect of intelligent men
and the love of little children;
who has filled his niche
and accomplished his task;
who has left the world better than he found it
whether by an improved poppy,
a perfect poem, or a rescued soul;
who has never lacked appreciation
of Earth's beauty

or failed to express it;
who has always looked for the best in others
and given them the best he had;
whose life was an inspiration;
whose memory a benediction.[94]

-Bessie Anderson Stanley,
American author 1904.

There have been disagreements through the years about who wrote, "Success," whether Ralph Waldo Emerson or Bessie Anderson Stanley. Robin Olson of robinsweb.com discusses her 2001 communications with Bessie Anderson Stanley's great-granddaughter, Bethanne Larson, who confirmed that her grandmother certainly wrote Success. It was stated that Mrs. Stanley won the Brown Book Magazine contest and a $250 cash prize for "Success". She used the money to pay the mortgage of her family home.[95]

---

[94] Stanley, Bessie Anderson. Success. Your Daily Poem. Com

[95] Olson, Robin. 2001. The Truth Behind Success in robinsweb.com

Addendum

Disruptors of Harmony has been a work in progress for many years. What began as journal entries during a difficult time in my life, grew into something larger. Through the years, writing has been a positive tool for me. It has helped me express my frustrations and satisfactions. It has given me an opportunity to revisit thoughts and feelings on paper. External factors and those which may be out of our control, may feel paralyzing and cause complications. Obstacles and thoughts of moving past them, may make one feel powerless or anxious. You are in control, and you have influence with your mind. You are the driver of your destiny. No other person or circumstance can take that from you. What you choose to think about and how you behave may make a positive difference.

It is important that we encourage positivity for ourselves and others. Take some time away from daily life stressors. Settle down with peaceful moments to decompress and relax. Understandably, this is not always easy, and you may say that there are not enough hours in a day. This is true; however, we must make time for even brief moments. Spend some time or even moments being with yourself and your environment. Efforts devoted to nature may bring forth serenity. Perhaps take a walk through the park and connect your spirit with the trees, flowers, grass, and even dirt. Weather conditions do not necessarily matter much. Try this during different weather conditions because it may lend to the experience. Perhaps consider the word "Alege" and think about its meaning, "to choose". It is your choice to embrace positivity, positive experiences, and positive affirmations. This will be your empowerment journey. It will assist you with ridding yourself of any disruptors of your harmony. Consider what brings you joy and tranquility. Reflect on appreciation and gratitude. May you have peace of mind and your days be filled with harmony! www.alegeempower.com

References

1. Merriam-Webster Dictionary in Merriam-Webster.Com, 2019.

2. Jefferson, Thomas. (March 4, 1801). University of Virginia, Miller Center, First Words:Thomas Jefferson.

3. Bacon, Francis. Brainyquotes.com, 2019

4. Wallis, C.; Mehrtens, R.,Thompson, D. (June 6, 1983). Time Magazine's, "Stress: CanWe Cope? Volume 121 (23): 48-54.

5. Nerurkar, A.; Bitton, A.; Davis, R.; Phillips, R.; and Yeh, G. Beth Israel Deaconess Medical Center. (2012, November 19). Stress Management Counseling in the Primary CareSetting is Rare. *ScienceDaily*. Retrieved November 21, 2019 from **www.sciencedaily.com/ releases/ 2012/11/121119163258.htm**

6. Robinson, Joe. (Updated July 22, 2013). Three-Quarters of Your Doctor Bills are Becauseof This. HuffPost in huffpost.com

7. Hatz-Seeley, Deborah. March 21, 2014. Chronic Stress is Linked to the Six LeadingCauses of Death. Miami Herald in Miamiherald.com

8. Wallis, et.al., (1983). 5.

9. Ibid

10. Ibid

11. Berczi, for Cannon, Walter (1932). Wisdom of the Body. United States: W.W. Norton &Company. ISBN 039300205511

12. Ibid

13. Wikipedia.org 2019

14. Wallis et al., (1983). 10

15. Ibid

16. Time Magazine- U.S. Edition. June 6, 1983. "Stress! Seeking Cures for ModernAnxieties. Vol. 121 No. 23

17. Cotton, Dorothy H.G. (1990). Stress Management: An Integrated Approach to Therapy.(Brunner/Mazel Psychosocial Stress Series): 3.

18. Seiz, Fred and Jonas, Bruce. Operational Definitions for Year 2000 Objectives: Priority Area 6, Mental Health and Mental Disorders. (1998). U.S. Dept. of Health and Human Services, Centers for Disease Control and Prevention, National Center for Health Statistics.

19. Freishtat, Alan. (2013). The Stress-Exercise Connection: How Does This Work? Orthodox Union.

20. Weissman, Judith, Ph.D.; Pratt, Laura A. Ph.D.; Miller, Eric A., Ph.D.; and Parker, Jennifer D., Ph.D. (2015). Serious Psychological Distress Among Adults: United States,2009-2013. NCHS Data Brief, No. 203, May 2015.

21. Washington Post. (January 23, 2007). "Facts on Stress"

22. Orman, Suze. June 29, 2017. Are You Ready to Declare Your Financial Independence? In suzeorman.com, Children, Family, Financial Independence, Saving.

23. Hall-Flavin, M.D., Daniel. Nov. 29, 2017. Can Chronic Stress Cause Depression? Healthy Lifestyle Stress Management in Mayoclinic.org.

24. Mayo Clinic.com 2/25/2010 Stress Management Can Chronic Stress Cause Depression?

25. Diagnostic and Statistical Manual of Mental Disorders, 4th Edition: DSM-4.

26. Merriam-Webster Dictionary in merriam-webster.com.

27. Gandhi, Mahatma by Tan, Chris. (17 March 2015). Mahatma Gandhi - Inspirational Quotes, Films, and Speech.

28. Gandhi, Mahatma. Wikipedia.com

29. Fema.gov, 4.1 General Information about Terrorism, page 148.

30. The Merriam-Webster Collegiate Dictionary, Tenth Edition.

31. Jefferson on Politics & Government: Inalienable Rights. ME 4:196, Papers 6:186

32. Federal Bureau of Investigations, Department of Justice.

33. Religioustolerance.org

34. U.S. Department of Health & Human Services, Office on Women's Health. (March 02,2018). Laws on violence against women.

35. Goodreads in goodreads.com, Confucius

36. Hunch.com

37. Malcolmx.com

38. Ibid

39. Ibid

40. Quotes.liberty-tree.ca

41. Quotation.cloud

42. Prize.org

43. Dictionary.com

44. Goodreads in goodreads.com

45. Quotes.liberty-tree.ca

46. Dictionary.com

47. Brainyquote.com

48. Gyatso, Kelsang. (April 1, 2012). Eight Steps to Happiness: The Buddhist Way ofLoving Kindness, Pages 3-4.

49. Contenderminitries.com

50. Religioustolerance.com

51. Quoteland.com

52. www.catholic -forum.com

53. Linehan, Marsha M., (1993). Skills Training Manual for Treating Borderline PersonalityDisorder, First Ed/Edition 1, 1993.

54. Witcraft, Forest, E in Quoteland.com

55. Prince George's County Public Schools in www.pgcps.org

56. Merriam-Webster.Com Dictionary

57. Azquotes.com

58. Biography.com

59. Sanders, Mark D., Sillers, Tia. (2000). I Hope You

Dance, Universal-MCA MusicPublishing, Inc., Tennessee.

60. Parks, Rosa. (August 20, 2019). Biography in Biography.com

61. King, brainyquotes.com62.Who2.com

63. Merriam-Webster.Com Dictionary

64. Wikipedia.org

65. EWTN.org

66. NOBELPRIZE.org67.Wikipedia.org

68. Diagnostic and Statistical Manual of Mental Disorders, 5th Edition: DSM-5.

69. Roosevelt, Eleanor. Eleanor Roosevelt Quote Page in home.att.net

70. Bookreporter.com

71. Goodreads in goodreads.com

72. Dictionary.com

73. Maraboli, Steve. (November 10, 2009). Life the Truth and Being Free, A Better TodayPublishing.

74. Suzy Kassem, Suzy. (May 15, 2011). Rise Up and Salute the Sun: The Writings of Suzy Kassem, Awakened Press.

75. Clausewitz, Gen. Carl Von, War, 1832.

76. Wagner, Glenmore (2019).

77. The 150 Most Important Bible Verses. (2007). Thomas Nelson, GRQ, Inc. Brentwood,Tennessee, page 145.

78. Cambridge Dictionary (2019)

79. Quoteland.com (2019)

80. Byrne, Rhonda. (2006). The Secret, Atria Books. Page 22.

81. McLean, Jamie, MD, Psychology with a Narcissistic Patient Using Kohut's SelfPsychology Model", Psychology (Edgmont) (2007 Oct.) Page 3.

82. Dumas, O'Hare Mary. (2019) Quoteland.com

83. Merriam-Webster.Com Dictionary

84. Good News Network, (October 17, 2018).

85. Chervin, Ronda De Sola. (1992). Quotable Saints. (St. Elizabeth Seton) page 102. CMJMarian Publishers, Oak Lawn, Illinois.

86. Green, David with High, Bill. (2017). Giving It All Away...and Getting It All BackAgain: The Way of Living Generously. Zondervan.

87. Merriam-Webster.Com Dictionary

88. Dalai Lama. (2002). How to Practic(Meaningful Life, His Holiness theDai lated and Edited by Jeffrey Hopkins, Ph..

89. Ibid

90. Ibid

91. Shimoff, Marci. Secrets of the Masters: The Missing Factor....Happiness

92. Team Clarizen. May 20, 2019. The Secret to Driving Change? Make NewBehaviors a Habit found in Clarizen Blog at Clarizen.com.

93. Cathy, S. Truett. BrainyQuote.com

94. Stanley, Bessie Anderson. Success. Your Daily Poem. Com

95. Olson, Robin. 2001. The Truth Behind *Success* in robinsweb.com

Made in the USA
Middletown, DE
24 March 2022